MOUNTAIN BIKING
Missoula

Dan Oko

FALCON®

GUILFORD, CONNECTICUT
HELENA, MONTANA

AN IMPRINT OF THE GLOBE PEQUOT PRESS

A FALCON GUIDE ®

Library of Congress Cataloging-in-Publication Data is available.

ISBN 0-7627-1156-6

Maps: Trapper Badovinac

Manufactured in the United States of America
First Edition/First Printing

Contents

Acknowledgments

There's no easy place to begin with regard to thanking the people who helped make this book possible. I apologize in advance for leaving anybody out. My heart belongs to Christina Willis, who patiently waited while I rode across the mountains of western Montana. Among those who rode with me and supplied recommendations for trails are Andrea Clark, Mike Schlafmann, Jeff "Stinky" Seaton, Rob Rusignola, Mike Warren, Tom Webster, Ken Picard, and Wayne Fairchild and the gang at Lewis and Clark Adventures.

Resources provided by Adventure Cycling and Low Impact Mountain Bicyclists of Missoula helped me get a handle on the scene when I first began riding in Missoula. For matters mechanical and additional recommendations, I also thank the folks at the Bike Doctor and Missoula Bicycle Works downtown. In addition, I would never have heard about this project if it weren't for Dan Dahlberg, owner of Open Road Bicycles. Please patronize these fine businesses—you'll find them and other bike shops listed in the back of this book.

My gratitude goes to Andy Kulla of the Lolo National Forest and former Missoula district ranger Dave Stack, who helped clarify the rules on access and keep me on the straight and narrow. I'd also like to thank Peggy O'Neill-McLeod, who not only shepherded the first chapters of this book but also provided me with an invaluable list of contacts down the line, and my editors, Erin Turner and David Singleton, who helped bring my long hours of riding and mapping to fruition with this volume.

Finally, it would have been impossible for me to survive in Missoula if it had not been for my tenure at the *Missoula Independent*. A hardy thanks to staff and management from 1994 to 1999.

Preface

For years mountain bikers in Missoula, Montana, have kept the quality of riding available in the Five Valleys a secret. With more than 1,800 miles of hiking and biking paths in the Lolo National Forest and backdoor trails leading to peaks of 8,000 feet and more, cyclists have been happy to allow the rest of the country to concentrate on such destinations as Moab, Utah, and Durango, Colorado—knowing that the riding in and around Missoula ranks it one of the top cycling cities in the nation. But while the locals have been guarded about letting the word get out about the Rattlesnake National Recreation Area and other favorite places, many cyclists in this neck of the woods have been waiting to let forth a barbaric "Yawp!" proclaiming Missoula one of the best biking towns anywhere: Consider this book that yawp.

Take it from me; I have ridden from coast to coast, from deep in the heart of Texas to the cloud-covered hills of the Pacific Northwest, and Missoula is one of those places mountain bikers dream of discovering. You can ride up huge hills of technical singletrack and enjoy scenic roads along mountaintop ridges or cruise streamside jeep trails and scream down intense downhills that rival any in the world. Keep your eyes open and you'll see elk and deer—maybe even a mountain lion or wolf. Pack a tent and spend the night under the stars in the Northern Rockies, where you might see the northern lights. Pack a rod and you can catch a wild trout—maybe even eat one for dinner, but don't be a glutton.

Truth be told, despite local efforts to keep things quiet, thousands of people have discovered not only the cycling opportunities in the Garden City, as Missoula is sometimes called, but also the fly-fishing, skiing, hiking, and camping opportunities that abound in western Montana. At the local college, the University of Montana, these recreational options have become a draw for young, athletic dreamers and future wildlife biologists at least as interested in exploring the outdoors as they are spending time in the classroom: Have bike will travel. But don't think these charms are lost on youth, because even full-fledged adults who have settled on Missoula as their place to buy a home, cultivate a career, and raise a family recognize, the qualities that make Missoula a dream town for outdoor adventurers—especially mountain bikers.

Of course, tension between newcomers and longtime residents can threaten to turn this dream into a nightmare. The locals will welcome you with open arms, provided you let them know that you are looking for experiences derived from appreciation and not exploitation. They'll share with you secret trails I have left out of this book—both those near town and the routes you'll find aways away—not to mention the best fishing holes and watering holes this side of the Bitterroot Divide. In exchange for that trust, Missoula's dedicated biking community will expect you to play by the rules, respect the wildlife, and honor the continuum of users that you may encounter when you're playing in both the front- and backcountry.

More than an ethical obligation, these local mores often reflect the literal law of the land. Across the country, access remains a hot topic of debate, and land managers in Missoula as elsewhere will continue to lock out mountain bikers who don't abide by the rules. Respect all closures, don't build or improve trails on public lands without agency approval, don't harass the wildlife, avoid trespassing on private land, and stay the heck out of the federally designated wilderness areas. Remember, even if you call Missoula home, always approach the trails as though you were a guest; respect other visitors and try to leave trails in better condition than you found them. These general rules will endear you to both the official and unofficial gate-keepers.

Which means more time for biking and less time for fighting—and that's a good thing, right? After all, if you're thumbing through this guide, you've got important things on your mind—like where you're going to ride. This is Missoula, and the choices are almost limitless. Get ready for a good time, and don't sweat keeping it a secret. The cat's out of the bag: Yawp!

P.S.: I have tried my best to make sure this book is accurate and up to date, but there will doubtless be changes to trails and access that come between now and whenever the first revisions take place. Please realize that trail conditions and access may change over time, and report any changes or errors to the publisher.

Map Legend

Interstate	(90)	Parking Area	**P**
US Highway	(55)	Railroad	┼┼┼┼┼┼┼┼┼
State Road	(555)	Campground	▲
Forest Road	416	Cabins/Buildings	■
Interstate Highway	⟹	Peak	🏔
Paved Road	⟹	Hill	⛰
Gravel Road	⟹	Cliffs	⟝⟞
Unimproved Road	===⟹	Berms	∿
Trailhead	◯	Gate	•—•
Ride	- - - - - - -	Bridge	⌣⌣
Trails/Footpaths	· · · · · ·	Cities	◉
Ride Direction	→ ⟋		
River/Creek	∿∿		
Spring	⟋	Map Orientation	N ↑
Lake	▬		
Picnic Area	⛩	Scale	0 ▬▬▬ Mile ▬▬▬ 1

Locator Map

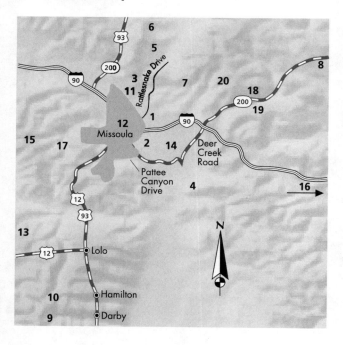

Get Ready to Crank!

Whether you've been tackling trails for years or you're planning your first ever mountain-bike ride, it's guaranteed that no matter how often you saddle up, the question persists: Where am I going to ride?

It's a question that experts must ask when their favorite local trails threaten to put them to sleep—and one that newcomers to the sport and Missoula must ask when they pull into the Garden City. But most of all, it's a question that I hope *Mountain Biking Missoula* will help answer—whether you're a longtime local or a short-time tourist, whether you ride once a week or once a year (even if you have never been on a ride before). There are nearly 1,800 miles of foot and bike paths in the Lolo National Forest alone, and this book represents a mere sampling of what's available in the Missoula area. Nonetheless, it should serve a full range of riders, from beginners to the most experienced, providing a starting point for adventurous cyclists of all stripes.

Mountain Biking Missoula looks at some of the best rides to be found in and around the city of Missoula, which is surrounded by public land in the form of national forests and federally designated recreation areas, and dotted with city and county parklands worth exploring. In these pages you'll find everything from technical ridgeline singletrack to scenic and smooth mountain roads to explore. Where possible I've described loops, although out-and-back runs and hilltop scrambles make up a few of the twenty rides you'll find here. Once you've conquered the outlined routes, you'll want to start mixing and matching courses. I'll make some recommendations (sometimes within the text of a specific ride), but the combinations are nearly endless, providing hundreds of miles of trails available for fat-tire fun.

The rides you'll find in *Mountain Biking Missoula* are described in simple language, with distances, technical difficulty, and physical challenges outlined clearly at the beginning of each ride. The book is small enough to fit in your hydration pack or saddlebag, and I hope you'll consider it a tool to take on the trail with you. The goal here is pretty basic: We want to help you select the right ride for your personal skill and conditioning level, get you to the trailhead without hassles, and ensure that you complete the ride safely without getting lost.

So what are you waiting for? I've taken the trouble to address that persistent question, now it's up to you to take advantage of the answer: Ride here now.

Getting Ready for
Missoula's Mountains

Missoula is nestled at the junction of five valleys, meaning there are hills galore just begging to bust you in your chops. The potential for fun is high, but there's no question that without solid skills and proper conditioning, the potential for trouble is also substantial. It's your responsibility to be prepared and to know your limits. You'll want to approach the offerings in *Mountain Biking Missoula* with a certain modesty. Unless you have acclimated to the altitude (remember, in Missoula climbing is king) and have a developed technique derived from hours in the saddle, you'll want to get a feel for some of the easier rides before tackling the lung busters and gnarly descents included in this guide.

Given the potential to get stuck in the woods, it's also important to make sure your bike is in good working order before hitting the trails. Before each ride, inspect your wheels, rims, and tires for damage; double-check your brakes; ensure that your shifters, and front and rear derailleurs are functioning correctly; look for looseness in the handlebars, headset, and seat and tighten where needed; and clean and lube your chain, checking for damage and stiff links. Also bring along a tool set with chain-break tool, a couple of Allen wrenches, a replacement tube or patch kit, tire levers, and an air pump—just in case something gives way during your ride. It goes without saying that you also need to know how to use these items. Walking your bike home in the dark when it's cold is a pretty lousy experience, especially when it can be avoided.

I also recommend bringing along at least one water bottle or hydration pack—certainly no less than sixteen ounces of liquid—some sort of high-calorie snack, foul-weather gear, sunglasses, lip balm, and insect repellent. If you don't know the drill, check with the friendly folks at any of Missoula's downtown bike shops; they'll get you out-fitted for a safe and hopefully pleasant ride. Remember, no matter what time of year it is, the weather can change in the mountains in just a few minutes, so follow the Boy Scout motto and be prepared. Snow in the late spring and early fall is not uncommon here.

As for cycling-specific clothing, I always recommend wearing a helmet. Head injuries are all too common for riders who don't wear the proverbial "brain bucket," and even if you're not worried about flipping over the handle-bars, a stray branch or a collision with an unexpected pine tree can do serious damage to the noggin. Eye protection is also crucial—not just from the sun's rays but also from the bugs and mud that can blind you on the trail. Gloves come highly recommended with regard to dressing for success: Gripping the handlebars with gravel embedded in your palms is just plain painful. Padded shorts can add to your comfort, and solid shoes that will allow you both to hike and bike should be required footwear in the mountains.

Finally, avoid riding alone. A buddy can be a lifesaver in the backcountry, and you never know when you're going to lose reception on that cell phone when you're hard-charging through the mountains. Likewise, before riding let a friend, family member, or neighbor know where you are going and when you plan on returning. Otherwise, res-cuers may have a hard time finding you or even knowing that you've disappeared.

Wildlife, Weather, and Wilderness

Basic mountain-bike ethics say that you should never harass wild animals. But in western Montana you also must remain mindful of what to do if wildlife —say, a bear or a lion—should decide to harass you. First off, this is Grizzly Country! While sightings of grizzly or brown bears are uncommon in this neck of the woods, grizzlies have been seen in recent years in the northern reaches of the Rattlesnake Recreation Area, along the Blackfoot River Recreation Corridor, and in the Ninemile Valley. More often than not, grizzlies will try to avoid you, but surprising a brown bear or coming between a mother bear—brown or black—and her cubs can mean trouble. The best response in these cases is not to take off riding or running. That could trigger the bear's instinct to chase, and grizzlies have been recorded running up to 40 miles per hour. So avoid the impulse to flee.

Rather, experts say that the best thing to do is slowly back away, keeping your arms down and speaking in a low, controlled voice while avoiding eye contact. In the case of a grizzly, definitely respect the bear's space and hope for the best. Black bears are more likely to be fearful of humans, so if one seems intent on attacking you, it may be worth yelling, throwing rocks, or even using your bike as a shield. Local wildlife authorities have literature that will enable you to learn the differences between brown and black bears (color is not always reliable). When it comes to mountain lion attacks, most adults don't have to worry, but make sure to protect small children. If you are confronted by a mountain lion, waving your arms and yelling will likely scare the big cat away. Once again, don't run—and remember that your bike can be used as a defensive weapon.

Missoula and its surrounding mountains receive weather sweeping down the west side of the Continental Divide and plenty of wetness from the Pacific Coast. The valley receives almost every sort of weather you can imagine, from sudden storms to scorching summer days to out-of-season snows in the late spring and early fall. In the mountains you even run the risk of flurries and freezing temperatures in July and August. Summer highs can reach 100 degrees; higher elevations tend to be cooler and breezier, while the mountains can "create their own weather," as they say, trapping storm clouds and bringing cold winds with no notice. As a rule, you will lose about 10 degrees for every 1,000 feet of elevation gain.

These factors can turn an enjoyable jaunt into a miserable slog, so in addition to bringing along a wind- or rainproof covering on the ride, consider bringing extra layers, leggings, and a change of clothes in the car if you're driving to the trailhead.

When it comes to riding in rain or snow or during spring runoff, conventional wisdom says that if you're leaving tracks, it's too wet to ride. Erosion and soil damage, combined with aesthetic concerns expressed by other users over rutted trails, make this a rule worth following. Plus likelihood of damage to your bike and body increases exponentially when you're cruising the wet roots and slick rocks stirred up in the Rocky Mountain gumbo. The popularity of snow biking has increased over the past few years, but winter cyclists should be courteous when it comes to cross-country ski trails and stay off groomed courses and skier tracks, especially up the Rattlesnake and in Pattee Canyon. The east front of Blue Mountain gets less snow and tends to recover more quickly from all kinds of precipitation, so the Blue Mountain National Recreation Area comes most recommended for those looking for four-season routes.

One of the joys of visiting Missoula (or living there) and exploring the surrounding recreation areas is the amount of public land, especially federal land, protected from development for cyclists, hikers, equestrians, and others to enjoy. This is a place where the phrase "Big Wild" has real resonance. Millions of acres of federally designated wilderness areas—such as the Rattlesnake Wilderness connected to the recreation area north of town, the Welcome

Creek Wilderness in the Sapphires, and the Bitterroot Wilderness southwest of Missoula—form an immense complex where human impact is kept to a minimum. Unfortunately for cyclists, these areas are not open for mountain biking, and while there has been much disagreement and discussion about the issue, it looks as though bikes will not be allowed to roam the federal wilderness anytime soon.

I agree with those who argue that bikes allow us to travel far enough and fast enough that it's appropriate to limit access with regard to wilderness areas, a sort of final frontier legislated to stay that way. If you disagree—and remember, we're discussing a legal matter here, so it's not really up for debate—with locking bikes out of the wilderness, there's still a very good reason to abide the law: If you don't, there's a good chance that mountain-bike access could be lost in areas adjacent to wilderness areas. In other words, if cyclists insist on ignoring this prohibition and "poaching" rides, we may find ourselves losing trails that are currently maintained with the cycling community at least partially in mind.

Another note of concern: Missoula has also seen a recent rash of nonsanctioned trails and construction projects, including bridgework and stunt areas, on public land. In many cases these projects are illegal and must be removed at taxpayer (read, *our*) expense. If they continue, it's more than likely that the powers that oversee public lands will begin to outlaw cycling in areas of concern. In the national forest and elsewhere, proposals for trail work—especially developing new trails and building obstacle courses—need to be evaluated according to environmental laws. If these laws continue to be broken, there is no question that access will be jeopardized. Future conflicts may be avoided if the cycling community moves to police itself.

Fat-Tire Ethics

We don't live in a perfect world, and cyclists cannot always be expected to police themselves.

Most of the laws imposed upon us, and most of the rules advocacy groups have come up with, reflect concern for the greater common good. If everyone abided by these regulations and suggestions, such as carrying out your trash and being courteous to your fellow users, there would be no need to even write these words. As it stands, the few, the proud, and the profoundly irresponsible—especially those who poach rides in wilderness areas, trespass on private property, and build new trails on public land without going through the proper, lawful channels—have left the rest of us to figure out how to ensure that mountain bikers in general are recognized as decent, fun-loving folks simply looking for a place to see the sights, get some exercise, and perhaps have a few thrills away from the huddled masses.

With thousands of miles of trail at stake, it's worth everybody reviewing the general guidelines for trail etiquette as suggested by the International Mountain Bike Association (IMBA)—recommendations shared by the local group, Low Impact Mountain Bicyclists of Missoula (LIMB). Many of these rules are common sense, their chief concerns being to promote environmental stewardship, to minimize negative impacts to land, water, plants, and animals, and to promote harmony on the part of all backcountry travelers—all of which should go a long way toward maintaining and even increasing trail access in the future. The following list has been adapted from IMBA and should refresh or familiarize you with the ABCs of what it means to be a responsible biker.

1. Respect closures. Ride only on open trails; if you're not sure, ask. Don't trespass on private land; stay out of areas where closures have been posted (wildlife protection and weather restrictions included). Remember, biking is not allowed in federal wilderness areas. Obtain permits for access or trailhead parking when necessary.

2. Leave no trace. This goes beyond packing out litter, including busted bike parts and wasted inner tubes. Don't leave ruts in muddy trails or ride in sensitive streambeds. Don't widen trails by riding around puddles. Stay off vegetation, and don't improve or construct trails or obstacles without authorization. Leave all gates how you find them (open or closed).

3. Control your bicycle and yield to fellow users. Ride within control, respecting all posted speed limits on the trail, and anticipate someone approaching at each blind bend. Avoid skidding around corners, and let others know when you're approaching. When passing horses and horseback riders, stand down and speak in a normal voice. Slow down when passing pedestrians. Make all interactions pleasant, no matter how brief.

4. Do not harass wildlife. Disturbing animals can be harmful to them—and to you. A startled moose or elk can present a serious obstacle. Slow down and make some noise, allowing all animals to get used to your presence. Never chase wildlife, and treat all livestock as you would wild animals, giving them wide berth and the chance to see or hear you and adjust. Do not run from predatory animals.

5. Know your limits. Be prepared to solve mechanical problems on the trail. Don't tackle technical rides if you don't have the requisite skill, and be aware of your level of physical conditioning before starting off on challenging trails. Dress appropriately and be prepared for changes in the weather. Bring adequate food and water. If you're riding in a group, be sure to communicate with your fellow riders about expectations. Let someone know where you're going and when you'll be back, and always wear a helmet.

Using This Guide

Mountain Biking Missoula is the result of more than four years of regular riding and a long hot summer of mapping routes in western Montana. There are twenty rides described in their entirety. In Appendix A, I have included a brief list of rides that have been documented elsewhere. Even with more time in the saddle, it would have been hard to pull together a comprehensive list of all the great trails the greater Missoula area has to offer, but this book makes an excellent starting place for beginners and is a good resource for old hands to get a handle on some new places to push them pedals. Many of the rides I have recorded as loops, although others can be broken up or recombined with other rides for nearly infinite combinations. In a few places I have broken out very brief connecting routes, which should be useful for beginners and families. Overall, there is a wide range of longer rides of varying difficulty described here.

The direction from which you approach many of these rides, especially the loops, will have a direct impact on the difficulty of the ride and, for some, whether you begin or end with a long run on pavement. I recommend first riding these trails as described and developing a sense of the terrain before tackling any of the rides from the opposite direction. Although this may appear the easier approach, that does not mean that the ride will not provide some serious challenges. In many cases weblike sets of singletrack surround the main routes described in *Mountain Biking*

Missoula. Most of these are fair game and have simply evolved over time as game trails and old jeep tracks have been explored by intrepid riders. Again, I recommend sticking to the route described before setting off on your own exploration—and remember to respect all closures.

The range of rides you'll find in this book is remarkable and reflective of the reason some people say that Missoula ought to rival Moab or Durango as a mountain-bike mecca. Some experienced technical masters may find this book a little tame, but I suspect that everybody who rides or intends to ride in Missoula will gain a better sense of the options in the region. A couple of rides stick pretty much to gravel roads and logging roads, and some people might argue that these selections do not rightly deserve to be rated alongside bona fide mountain-bike trails. To you critics (real or imagined) I say, relax: This is a book intended for a broad range of people. I have ridden trail from Seattle to Austin to Boston and can tell you that the most fun I ever had on a bike was riding for this book.

That said, mountain biking doesn't always need to be about pain. Stop and smell the flowers. Think in terms of active rest. Or get out there and hammer any one of the valley-to-peak loops, enjoy climbing singletrack and the burn of your lungs and thighs before snaking through the forest on a major downhill, then back to the trailhead along a sparkling creek where trout flash. Whatever your preference, I hope you'll find this volume suits your needs.

Each ride uses the same descriptive format:

Ride number and name should help you cross-reference the rides in this book. In many cases rides can be linked together for extra loops and extensions, providing longer trips for those not worn down by the initial offerings. Usually the text of the ride notes "see Ride #." The names are usually derived from the trails followed or the destination, geological features, or high point of a given ride. In some cases I have used the local nickname for the ride; generally, if the ride is a loop, that also has been included in the title.

Location tells where the ride is located in relation to Missoula and the direction it travels. In many cases the trailhead can be reached by riding from downtown; if the ride is out of town, this section will indicate how far and in what direction.

Distance is the length of the ride. I have noted whether this measures a loop, one-way, or round-trip.

Time should be counted as an estimate of how long it takes to complete the trip. The time listed pertains only to the duration you should expect to be in the saddle; breaks for rest, maintenance, or other reasons have not been included. (It's worth noting that in mapping the rides, I was forced to stop often, which kept my average speed low.) Stronger riders may well be able to ride a given route faster than the time I recorded; new and slower riders, especially those unfamiliar with the terrain, should realize that it may take them a little longer. Weather, trail conditions, mechanical difficulties, and other variables can add considerable time to your ride.

Tread describes the type of trail or road covered by the ride—singletrack, doubletrack, jeep roads, logging roads, gravel roads, and paved roads. In some cases trail "deterioration" such as erosion and vegetation can turn jeep tracks and logging roads into doubletrack and even singletrack, while trail improvements may make some former singletrack more like gravel roads.

Aerobic level is rated as easy, moderate, or strenuous (with some room for variation). This pertains to the physical challenge and conditioning demands for each ride. Easy refers to flat and rolling terrain; moderate terrain has some hills, both short and steep and long and gradual, but nothing that practiced mountain-bike riders should find too painful; strenuous includes long, steep climbs and will generally require serious aerobic conditioning. Remember, if you find yourself exhausted and out of gears, walking is always an option—as some people say, "It ain't a mountain-bike ride until you get off and walk." Also keep in mind that altitude can impact even the most fit riders.

Technical difficulty rates the obstacles from Level 1 to Level 5, using the highest level of challenge as the overall measure. In other words, most of a ride may be rated Level 2, meaning that the terrain has some rough spots but is mostly a smooth, wide trail. If a steep section of rocky ledges comes at the end of a ride, even if it only accounts for a short distance, I will rate the ride Level 3 or 4, depending on the most difficult obstacles you can expect to face. The breakdown follows:

 Level 1: Smooth; paved or gravel road. Requires no technical handling skills, just basic knowledge of how to ride a bike.

 Level 2: Mostly wide and smooth tread; perhaps doubletrack or wide singletrack with small ruts, loose rock or gravel, and other minor obstacles that could give children or newcomers to the sport a little—but very little—trouble.

 Level 3: Tread fluctuates between rough, bumpy, and occasional smooth sections of bona fide singletrack and doubletrack marked by more substantial obstacles, such as large rocks and fallen branches. At this level the trail options will always be obvious, although suspension such as front-fork shock absorbers may be helpful. Sharp turns, steep switchbacks, deep ruts, and water bars add potential challenges.

 Level 4: Nothing smooth about it; you'll take your lumps as you traverse varied, primarily singletrack terrain.

Climbs and descents will tend to be steep and littered with larger rocks, roots, and the like, requiring extensive handling abilities. Off-camber, nonhorizontal sections of trail, narrower tread, and fewer course options add to the challenge, as do deeper ruts and numerous obstacles, including stream crossings.

Level 5: Extremely rough single- and doubletrack marked by continuous obstacles, ranging from rocks and roots to ledges, jumps, drop-offs, exposed hillside riding, boulders, logs, and water crossings. The trails at this level tend to be narrower—the climbs and descents not only steeper but also alternating in quick succession—and require plenty of experience for safe negotiations.

Again, remember that the rides in this book tend to have some variation and have been rated not for the predominant level or terrain, but for the most challenging. The only way to be able to tackle the bigger obstacles is to practice, so read the ride descriptions carefully. When you think you are getting the feel for things at a certain level, consider attempting a new trail that has received a slightly higher rating. Use your gearing to your advantage by exploring different settings that may allow you to keep pedaling and riding over various types of obstacles. Riding with more experienced cyclists will also allow you to glean tips on how to overcome the challenges you face on the trail.

Highlights provides a general ride description to determine the reasons for doing a certain ride—outside of getting out and having some downright fun. Here you'll find recommendations for seasons, additional nearby scenic attractions, fishing holes, and other items of interest, including potential hookups with other trails (see Ride #).

Land status refers to managing agencies and land owners. Many of the rides in this book are on national forest land, including Pattee Canyon, the Rattlesnake, and Blue Mountain Recreation Area in Lolo National Forest. In some cases land is managed by or belongs to State of Montana agencies, the city of Missoula or Missoula County, private companies such as Plum Creek Timber Company, and occasionally private individuals. Do not trespass if you do not have explicit permission, stay out of designated federal wilderness areas and other public holdings that have closures, and no matter who owns the property you traverse (or your feelings about said owners), respect the land itself. (See Appendix B for public agency contacts.)

Maps lists the official or agency maps that can help you find your way. In the cases of federal recreation areas, basic maps are available at the trailhead and at the Forest Service Region 1 Headquarters in Missoula (see Appendix B). More specifically, I have listed USGS maps from the 7.5-minute quad series, certainly the most detailed maps available for most of the rides. They can be purchased at outdoor shops in Missoula and elsewhere. Where appropriate I have included other resources, including Bureau of Land Management and Forest Service maps.

Access explains how to find the trailhead or start of the ride. I have tried to indicate for each ride whether it is best to bike or drive to this point. Many of the rides can be reached from downtown with a little extra pedaling.

The ride provides a detailed breakdown by distance of key points such as landmarks, significant obstacles, trail intersections, and changes in geology and topography. Other noted items in the description include stream crossings, major turns, scenic overlooks, and tread changes along the ride. The distances were measured with a bike-mounted computer—a notoriously inaccurate way of determining distance—and rounded to the nearest tenth of a mile, so please consider these measurements an estimate. Nonetheless, combined with the use of a topographic map and compass, following these directions is your best bet for staying on the right trail.

On a final note, trails change from season to season, and management agencies and landowners regularly change policy on access. At the other end of the spectrum, cycling groups such as LIMB and IMBA regularly improve trails and occasionally build new ones. That said, mountain biking is a risky sport, and riders must be prepared to take responsibility for themselves. I have tried to be as current as possible in my ride descriptions, but if you'd like to report any problems or noteworthy changes to any of these routes, please contact the publisher.

Elevation profile provides a graph for nearly every ride description. The ups and downs of the route are pictured on a chart that measure mileage and height above sea level, in feet. The surface conditions of the road and, in some cases, the technical level of each section of ride are shown. The graphs are not done to scale, and the lines on the graphs are generally not as steep as the slope of the hill; although at some point, you will note a level of correlation. In some cases, because of the size of the graph, you may experience some climbs and dips not transcribed in these profiles, but you will read about almost all of them in the ride description.

Subjectively Speaking

All the descriptions in this book are based on my experience riding the trails in and around Missoula, sometimes alone, but often with friends. My skills—despite covering nearly a thousand miles in a summer of mapping—do not place me in the crème de la crème of cyclists. I'm a strong rider but not fast, and my skills were still developing when I accepted the assignment to write *Mountain Biking Missoula*. I mention this because it's up to each rider to know his or her own limits when it comes to heading out on the trail. I've tried to include something for everybody, but certainly some folks will complain that the rides I've chosen are not challenging enough, while others will argue that many of these routes are far too advanced. The key is to sample a few and use what you find as a measure for what you can expect the next time out, according to this guide

If you have not figured it out yet, you will also soon realize that mountain biking is not like other sports. Its emergence as one of the fastest growing outdoor activities has prompted an evolution in parts and materials that would give NASA scientists pause. I tackled the trail on a chromoly steel hardtail with a midlevel front shock. As I have mentioned, I am not particularly fast, and my bike was not particularly light. My claim to fame during my years riding in Missoula has been that I can almost always keep up. But sometimes, to this day, I can be found just a little off the back, hanging on to the handlebars for dear life. If you have some experience with mountain bikes, you may know where you sit in the overall spectrum of riders, and you may know what you are capable of tackling with the ride you've picked out. If not . . . read on.

Mountain biking adds a lot of rough-and-tumble action to the world of cycling. It's most fun done with friends, and the wide choice in equipment means that you will probably have a chance to try out several different types of bikes before settling on a favorite to carry you over the long haul. In the meantime, there is no shame in taking a rest or walking your bike sometimes. Start out with short training rides, and build up to the longer more technical routes. Remember, especially when it comes to technical trails, even the best riders occasionally are forced to dismount. Some prefer to be thrown headfirst over the handlebars—a maneuver called an "endo" or "superman" in cycling parlance—while others simply stop their bikes and step off more or less gracefully. Again, as you gain experience you will doubtless have the chance to decide which sort of experience you prefer.

That about covers it from this end. Remember, when you ride you represent all other mountain bikers. Be courteous and lawful, wear a helmet, strive to be inconspicuous, and clean up after yourself. And above all, have fun.

U.S. West Access–
Marshall Canyon Loop

Location: Mount Jumbo on the east edge of Missoula.

Distance: 11.1-mile loop.

Time: 1 hour.

Tread: Mixed single- and doubletrack with some pavement.

Aerobic level: Moderately strenuous.

Technical difficulty: Between Levels 2 and 3 with a 4-plus–rated section on the exposed front of Mount Jumbo, which also features a couple of steep switchbacks.

Highlights: Views of the Clark Fork River Valley east of Missoula reward those able to conquer the mountain not just once, but twice. Mount Jumbo has plentiful wildlife, including a resident elk herd. Since 1997 Mount Jumbo has been a cornerstone of Missoula's open-space plan. This means portions of the hill that this ride encompasses will never be developed. In order to retain access, cyclists—as well as skiers and hikers—must respect seasonal closures intended to protect the resident elk herd during winter months and calving season.

Land status: Montana Fish, Wildlife, and Parks; Missoula Open Space; Lolo National Forest; and some land in the Marshall Canyon owned by Plum Creek Timber Company.

•U.S. West Access–
Marshall Canyon Loop

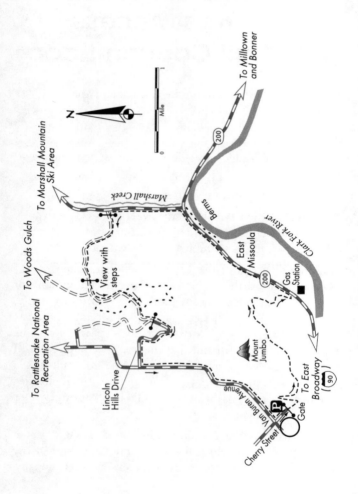

Maps: USGS Northeast Missoula, USGS Northwest Missoula, USGS Blue Point, and Lolo National Forest. Maps of Mount Jumbo area are also posted at the Cherry Street trailhead and mountaintop gates.

Access: Ride from town to the Cherry Street access to Mount Jumbo in the lower Rattlesnake neighborhood just off Van Buren Avenue, or head for Lincoln Hills Drive farther north (off Rattlesnake Drive) and ride to Jumbo's saddle, tackling the circuit backwards. By car, head north from the junction of Van Buren Avenue and East Broadway, taking the underpass below I–90 (if you're on the highway, turn north once you get off at the Van Buren exit), and drive 3 blocks, taking a right onto Cherry Street. After 2 blocks you'll see parking, a gate, and the trailhead straight ahead.

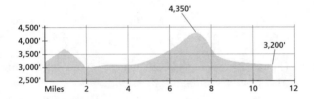

The Ride

0.0 Take Van Buren Avenue, traveling north from East Broadway, across from the University of Montana footbridge, and make a right on Cherry Street after riding 2 blocks to reach the entry gate where the street ends. Park here if driving. Take note of any special closures.

0.3 Stick to the right, heading uphill and parallel to I–90 and the Clark Fork River, along dirt and loose-rock singletrack.

0.8 Finish ascent; follow the power lines across the face of the mountain.

1.1 Begin descent; keep your eyes open for where the trail cants away from the hillside, as well as for a few mildly technical switchbacks.

1.6 Stay left, riding around the trees instead of dropping down the eroded drop-off, then hit a steep switchback that will take you down to the pavement. From here on out, stay right.

1.8 On the edge of East Missoula, you reach an empty lot just off Highway 200, which is crossed by Heighton Road. Watch for traffic. Take a left on Highway 200 to reach Marshall Mountain. (Turning right will carry you back to Missoula proper and East Broadway.)

3.2 On your right large berms overlook the Clark Fork River and offer a bit of stunt riding off the pavement. Otherwise, ride in the drainage ditch or on the road.

4.0 Cross pavement at ski area sign on your left; climb road towards Marshall Mountain.

5.0 Take left at gate onto Plum Creek Timber Company land; begin climbing jeep track.

5.7 Marshall Grade turnoff is on your right; stay left. The pullout offers a great view of the valley as well as the Milltown Dam, which keeps all sorts of toxic mine waste in place.

6.0 Reenter open-space area on Mount Jumbo, using the wooden steps to circumvent the gate. Again, note specific closures and keep an eye open for other users.

6.2 Steep trail to Marshall Grade (see Ride 7). Stay on main trail, keeping left.

6.4 Take right onto vague jeep trail.

7.1   Take left, heading downhill toward the gate and off the saddle to the west.

7.3   Skirt gate and pick up dirt road, heading left toward downtown (or right toward the upper Rattlesnake neighborhood and other rides).

7.4   Return to pavement at the top of Lincoln Hills Drive, a steep and winding road. Stay on Lincoln Hills Drive, being careful of traffic and pedestrians, until it flattens out and carries you to Rattlesnake Drive.

8.9   Take left on Rattlesnake Drive, heading south and toward town. Watch for traffic.

10.9   Take a left on Cherry Street; ride 2 blocks.

11.1   Reach starting gate and parking area at trailhead.

Deer Creek–
Pattee Canyon Loop

Location: From the University of Montana around the backside of Mount Sentinel east of Missoula, returning to town through the Pattee Canyon Recreation Area to the South Hills neighborhood.

Distance: 17.2-mile loop.

Time: 2 hours, 15 minutes.

Tread: Primarily gravel and logging roads with a brief section of singletrack.

•Deer Creek–
Pattee Canyon Loop

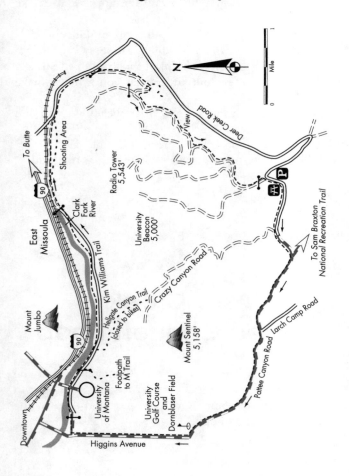

Aerobic level: Moderately strenuous.

Technical difficulty: Mostly Level 2, with a very brief 3-plus-rated-section running above some railroad tracks in Hellgate Canyon. Pattee Canyon Road, which is paved, rates a 2 because it's steep and curvy.

Highlights: The scenic Kim Williams Trail runs along the Clark Fork River, joining this ride with Missoula's urban trail system. Wildflowers and wildlife reside on the backside of Mount Sentinel, which continues to regenerate following extensive logging by Champion Timber Company. The winding climb affords views of the clear-cut, burnt, and pristine forest sections that form the land matrix throughout the region. Pattee Canyon Recreation Area draws a wide range of recreationists and offers excellent picnic spots and shaded areas for resting following the climb, as well as additional cycling loops. Coming down the blacktop provides its own rush, although traffic concerns call for caution.

Land status: City of Missoula, Missoula County, Plum Creek Timber Company, and Lolo National Forest.

Maps: USGS Southeast Missoula and Lolo National Forest.

Access: The Kim Williams Trail, which marks the starting point, can be accessed at several points along the south bank of the Clark Fork River in downtown Missoula. Some parking spots can be found both immediately east and west of the Higgins Avenue Bridge. (Mileage has been calculated starting from the University of Montana footbridge just north of campus, which runs over the river and into Van Buren Avenue as it crosses East Broadway.)

Special note of concern: Although most users of the Kim Williams Trail have no problems, the area along the river just east of campus is frequented by transients, and at least

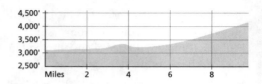

one woman was attacked there in recent years. Female riders in particular may want to avoid riding this loop alone.

The Ride

0.0 Begin ride, heading east from the University of Montana footbridge into the mouth of Hellgate Canyon along the Kim Williams Trail. University buildings should be on your right.

0.2 Reach gate, which can be circumvented to the right. You'll soon see the footpath to M Trail on the right; continue on Kim Williams Trail, going straight.

0.8 A network of footpaths, sometimes shared with cyclists, is on the left; no turn.

1.2 Hellgate Canyon Trail, a footpath (no biking), is on the right; no turn.

3.0 Ride around gate to right and continue right up vague jeep trail; do not follow trail along railroad tracks. This becomes singletrack shortly.

3.4 Beyond the fence on your right (north), a road appears. This is the Deer Creek Shooting Area, a privately maintained target range. You may hear shots. Do not be alarmed; keep riding.

3.6 Trail narrows to only true technical point. The singletrack follows the deep railroad cut for about 0.25 mile.

3.8 Begin brief descent.

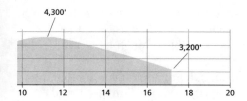

4.0 Berm separates rider from Deer Creek Road; take a right on road, passing gate for shooting area, on the way to begin climb. (A left carries you to East Missoula, which is an early-season option before the snow has come off the hill.)

4.3 Start climbing Deer Creek Road.

5.1 Take right to gate and go around, picking up old logging road and leaving Deer Creek Road behind. Take first road to left (southwest) and begin steady climb among spruce and aspen.

6.1 On left, see vague, knapweed-choked road; bear right and keep climbing.

6.2 Directly in front, a clearing opens up; keep on the road, switchbacking uphill to right.

6.6 See gate ahead; climb up switchback on your left.

6.9 Road flattens out for a period, providing views of clear-cuts and burns across the way; take a few easy turns along the road as it crosses the mountain face in a southwesterly direction. Resume climbing.

8.5 A road enters from the right; keep the course, staying left. (A right on this road will take you the radio tower.)

9.3 Connect to Jeep Trail, which heads up to University Beacon; take a left (south).

9.4 Doubletrack appears on right; continue straight on main road until you emerge at Pattee Canyon Recreation Area. The landscape opens up. Frisbee golfers, dog walkers, and picnickers come together amidst the parklike stands of ponderosas.

9.7 Ahead, parking is visible through trees; bear left on trail.

10.0 See fence; take right to fork, take another right, then take a final right onto the unpaved road.

10.2 Reach pavement. This is Pattee Canyon Road. Watch for traffic. On your left you'll see a No Entry sign and parking. This marks the start of Sam Braxton National Recreation Trail (see Ride 4), which can be found at the head of the lot.

10.3 Parking and Pattee Canyon Picnic Area are on right.

11.1 Lower Pattee Canyon parking is on right.

14.5 Enter lower Pattee Canyon residential area. Slow down, keeping an eye open for cars.

14.7 Reach stop sign and take a right onto Higgins Avenue, heading north. Pass the University Golf Course and Dornblaser Field.

16.2 Take right off Higgins Avenue and onto Fourth Avenue, heading east toward Hellgate Canyon.

16.6 Reach Kim Williams Trail; continue straight ahead. (Or head home or to wherever you parked your car.)

17.2 Kim Williams Trail reaches the University of Montana footbridge.

Sawmill–
Curry Gulch Loop

Location: Rattlesnake National Recreation Area just north of Missoula.

Distance: 5.9-mile loop.

Time: 45 minutes.

Tread: Singletrack, jeep trails, and a small stretch on a vehicle-free gravel road on the way in and out.

Aerobic level: Moderate–moderately strenuous.

Technical difficulty: Level 3 with one stretch of 3 plus as you descend Curry Gulch to Spring Gulch, a little past the halfway point.

Highlights: The Sawmill–Curry Gulch Trail System forms the heart of some of Missoula's best mountain biking (not to mention hiking). This ride offers a great opportunity to become acquainted with the topography and landscape that makes Missoula an unsung mecca of mountain biking in the Northwest. Still, the Sawmill-Curry Gulch Loop sees a lot of usage and should be explored—if possible—on weekdays and other times when it's not teeming with visitors. Or try to use the route as a launching pad for other easily accessible loops. On this ride you'll see where some of the valley's original homesteaders laid down roots, and if you get to it early enough in the season, you'll beat the knapweed that has invaded the Rattlesnake ecosystem and enjoy greenery throughout the trip.

Sawmill–Curry Gulch Loop

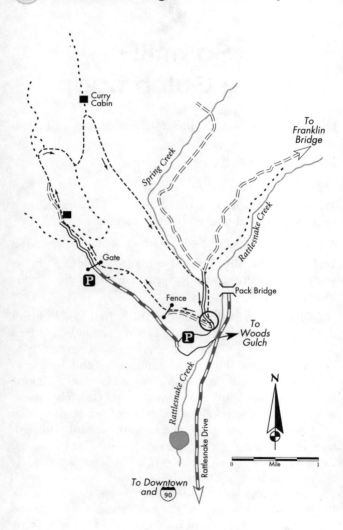

Land status: The entire loop is on national forest land within the Rattlesnake National Recreation Area.

Maps: USGS Northeast Missoula, Lolo National Forest, and the Sawmill-Curry Trail System map (available at the trailhead or Forest Service Region 1 Heaquarters in town). A permanent map of the entire Rattlesnake National Recreation and Wilderness Area is installed at the trailhead.

Access: Driving, follow Van Buren Avenue to Rattlesnake Drive from East Broadway, or take the Van Buren exit off I–90 and head north. You can also ride the Rattlesnake Greenway from downtown (see Ride 11 for directions). Take a right after 2.5 miles, staying on Rattlesnake Drive, and then a left after about 4 miles once the drive starts to snake through the woods. Here you will see a sign for the Rattlesnake Main trailhead; follow the road over the bridge that straddles Rattlesnake Creek and bear right to the main parking lot.

Special note of concern: Like much of the region, the Rattlesnake National Recreation Area has fallen prey to noxious weeds. During the spring the Forest Service undertakes an aggressive herbicide campaign in Sawmill Gulch to fight knapweed and leafy spurge. If you're chemically sensitive or riding with children, you may want to check with the Missoula Ranger District before heading out. You'll also want to avoid transporting seeds from this area to others and vice versa; be sure to clean your bike before and after riding.

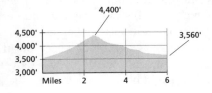

The Ride

0.0 Starting from the parking lot, you can either ride 0.75 mile or so up the paved road, where you'll see a fence on your right, or take the Rattlesnake Main Trail 99, passing the map stand and picking up a jeep trail. I recommend the latter route.

0.2 From Trail 99, take a left-hand turn around the tree onto the doubletrack and start climbing. This carries all the way to Sawmill Gulch as you pedal through a shaded section of thick conifers that offers rolling singletrack that swoops through the woods with gentle exertion and some technical challenges.

0.7 See fence and road, pedaling hard to get over the roots and such as you head for the singletrack on right.

0.9 Bear left, continuing through the trees. Although you're steadily gaining a bit of altitude, enjoy the dips in the trail.

1.4 A path to your left reconnects with the road, which you should be able to see. Keep to your right for the last bit of singletrack.

1.6 Push up the last bit of road and find yourself in the upper parking lot. Head around the fence through the notch on the left and start climbing the dirt road. No vehicle traffic allowed here.

1.9 A sharp right will carry you up to the Curry-Sawmill junction, but you'll probably have to walk at some point. Instead, stay left and keep pedaling up to the homestead foundations along the road.

2.1 Ride over the cement floor, check out the ruins all around, then continue until you see the singletrack up to the slight bench on your left. Take the first or second track, up the steep section, and bank right. Continue climbing in the rutted doubletrack.

2.5 Take the well-worn cutoff on your right, pushing hard up another steep section, then turn right again on the old road. Keep on the main trail as it winds uphill through the pine forest. Late in the season is the time you're most likely to see wildlife, especially deer.

3.0 Reach the axis of Sawmill and Curry Gulches. On your right, through the trees, you'll see where the trail that you passed at mile 1.9 reconnects with this loop. To your left, numerous trails branch out. Follow the sign to Curry Gulch, heading north by northwest, and take the first left onto Curry Trail 282 beginning your descent.

3.5 Pick up Curry Trail 281 on your right (Curry Trail 282 continues, carrying you toward Curry Cabin, a worthwhile side trip), and descend along a moderately challenging section of singletrack marked by rubber water bars. Watch for plenty of ruts, rocks, and roots.

4.3 The trail smoothes out and snakes through the trees for about 0.3 mile. Watch for pedestrians.

4.4 Coming out of the woods, you'll hook up with Spring Gulch and other loops. Take a right here, heading southeast on Stuart Peak Trail 517 along excellent singletrack. Watch for water berms and more people. The band of trees on your left marks the spring, and the poplars are mostly what's left of the homesteaders in this valley.

4.6 Ride back into the woods for a little over 0.1 mile. Roots and rock gardens abound, so beware.

5.4 Reach Rattlesnake Main Trail 99, which carries north to Franklin Bridge (see Ride 5) and south to the main trailhead. Go right, heading downstream, and remember that there's a 10 mph speed limit. Be courteous and safe along this gravelly, vehicle-free road.

5.7 The jeep trail rising on your right should provide a sense of déjà vu. The map stand is just ahead, also on the right.

5.9 Finish ride; you're back at the main Rattlesnake parking lot.

Sam Braxton National Recreation Trail

Location: The Pattee Canyon Recreation Area on the east edge of Missoula.

Distance: 2.5-mile loop.

Time: 30 minutes.

Tread: Singletrack.

Aerobic level: Moderate.

Technical difficulty: Level 2+.

Highlights: Named for a longtime Missoula rider and bike shop owner, the Braxton loop is an excellent beginners' route. It's also short enough to be a fine after-work jaunt when daylight is failing. A challenging circuit without too

•Sam Braxton National Recreation Trail

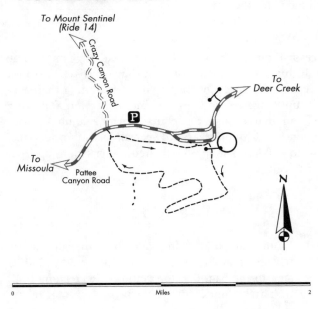

To Mount Sentinel
(Ride 14)

Crazy Canyon Road

To
Deer Creek

P

To
Missoula

Pattee
Canyon Road

N

0   Miles   2

many serious obstacles, it's an excellent place for intermediate riders to work on their bike-handling skills. Shaded
by pines and occasional aspens, the forest floor bears a
multitude of wildflowers through the height of summer;
deer, rodents, and birds call these woods home as well.

Land status: Lolo National Forest, closed yearlong to
motorized vehicles.

Maps: USGS Northeast Missoula and Lolo National Forest.
There is a cross-country ski trail map that shows a route

near the entrance. The Forest Service Region 1 Headquarters has a trail guide for the Pattee Canyon Recreation Area.

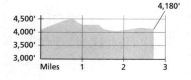

Access: From downtown Missoula, take Higgins Avenue south to the junction with Pattee Canyon Drive, just past the University Golf Course on your left. Riding the pavement up Pattee Canyon Drive is another option, following the road that is also the course for the annual Pattee Canyon Hill Climb each fall. Especially strong riders may want to make this loop a final circuit after riding up from Deer Creek (see Ride 2).

The Ride

0.0 From east parking lot, ride through gate, across pavement, and to second gate, where you will see a sign to the Sam Braxton National Recreation Trail. Bear right, notice the ATTENTION MOUNTAIN BIKERS rule sign on left, and start climbing singletrack to right of the signed Southside Ski Trail.

0.1 As you approach the first 0.1 mile, a sharp right will carry you up a very steep but brief hill. An arrow showing the way and a national recreation trail plaque nailed to a tree are visible from the trail. Follow trail between two ponderosa pines, and bear left up hill.

0.2 A singletrack comes in from right, but bear left and follow the arrows as you climb. Take another right, entering a modest technical stretch.

0.3 Follow arrow, marking a left turn.

0.4 Instead of continuing on the trail directly ahead, take a left.

0.5 Bear right, following three arrows showing designated route—just a little more climbing.

0.6 Begin descent, but be ready for minor but steep switchback.

0.7 Climb steep, short hill. Shortly, an abandoned jeep track enters the trail. Stay on singletrack and continue descent.

0.8 Follow a single switchback; keep an eye out for the arrow marker on the fence post.

0.9 Another old jeep track, even more overgrown, comes in from the right. Keep on singletrack.

1.2 Spot another arrow; bear left and continue descending.

1.3 Dip, then climb, and get prepared for a brief but technical descent.

1.4 Wide switchbacks form an S-curve descent.

1.6 You're coming up on a fork in the road; take the right, which leads to a viewpoint of alternating forested and logged hills across the way to the west.

1.7 Ahead, a blue arrow marks the ski trail; stay left, following silver arrow for the Sam Braxton National Recreation Trail. A T-stop is also marked by dueling arrows; again follow the silver arrow to left, continuing down a short, steep section of trail.

1.9 The road forks. Take a right (left carries you to Pattee Canyon Road), climb to right, and meet up with singletrack headed up from road below. Keep right.

2.1 One more overgrown jeep track intersects the trail.

2.2 Take left, then right, following sign and arrow to the trailhead. Pass an outhouse on your right and picnic tables on your left as you head back toward the parking area.

2.3 Meet up with Southside Ski Trail and start of loop. Head out stem on left.

2.5 Return to parking lot.

Main Corridor of Rattlesnake, Franklin Bridge and Beyond

Location: Rattlesnake National Recreation Area north of downtown.

Distance: 8.4 miles one-way to Franklin Bridge; 15 miles one-way to wilderness boundary; 30 miles round-trip.

Time: 1 hour, 20 minutes round-trip to Franklin Bridge; 3 hours, 15 minutes round-trip to wilderness boundary.

Tread: Gravel road, jeep track, and occasional doubletrack.

Aerobic level: Strenuous.

Technical difficulty: Level 2.

Highlights: Once the most popular trail in Missoula, the arduous climb from the Rattlesnake Main trailhead to the wilderness boundary still draws quite a few visitors. But because of bike technology and a proliferation of trails throughout the area, some use has been mitigated. Still,

•Main Corridor of Rattlesnake, Franklin Bridge and Beyond

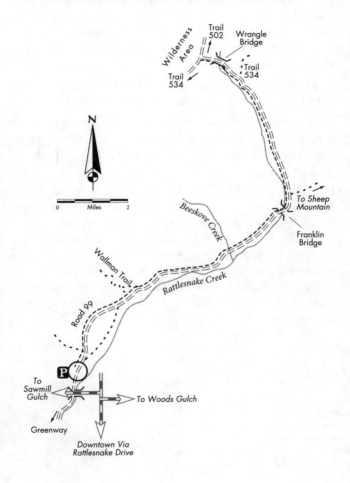

this ride, while supremely bumpy, captures much of what's great about Missoula riding; it carries riders along a meandering old ranch road from low mountain meadows to the pine forests protected forever from human development (and invading cyclists) by dint of its wilderness designation. Rattlesnake Creek still has a lively fishery, which can be fished above Beeskove Creek. Franklin Bridge is entirely accessible for novice riders.

Land status: The entire loop is on national forest land within the Rattlesnake National Recreation Area.

Maps: USGS Northeast Missoula and Lolo National Forest. A permanent map of the entire Rattlesnake National Recreation and Wilderness Area is installed at the trailhead.

Access: Driving, follow Van Buren Avenue to Rattlesnake Drive from East Broadway, or take the Van Buren exit off I–90 and head north. You can also ride the Rattlesnake Greenway from downtown (see ride 11 for directions). Take a right after 2.5 miles, staying on Rattlesnake Drive. and then a left after about 4 miles once the drive starts to snake through the woods. Here you will see a sign for the Rattlesnake Main trailhead; follow the road over the bridge that straddles Rattlesnake Creek, and bear right to the main parking lot.

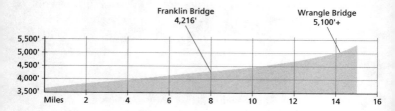

The Ride

0.0 The main trailhead to Rattlesnake National Recreation Area, there's a permanent map and sign board just beyond the gated entrance as you head up the gravel road, Road 99, which parallels the creek. After 0.25 mile, beyond an old jeep trail on the left (see Ride 3), this trail skirts a rock wall on your left. Watch for pedestrians and keep under the posted speed limit!

0.4 The valley opens up. The pack bridge from the horse trailhead will be on the right; a sign on the left indicates mileage and various trails. Follow signs for Franklin Bridge and wilderness boundary along Road 99.

0.6 Singletrack spurs appear in succession on the right and left. To avoid user conflict, stay on main road, which climbs gradually and enters the woods.

0.8 Pass another singletrack spur and outhouse on right as you bear left on Road 99.

2.0 See sign for Wallman Trail and Spring Gulch on left (see Ride 6). Stay on main road, which continues to get rockier from here on out.

2.5 Singletrack on right enters the trail.

2.6 A second, small wooden sign for Wallman Trail and Spring Gulch is on left.

3.5 A Forest Service outhouse is on the right as you reach the end of the 3-mile zone, inside of which camping, shooting, and other activities are prohibited. The adventurous may want to bring a tent and camp along here.

6.6 Cross Beeskove Creek. (Fishermen can try their luck in Rattlesnake Creek above this point.)

8.4 Reach Franklin Bridge. This is an excellent turn-around point for those who want to head back to the trailhead, although continuing on just a little farther opens up views of the north end of the Rattlesnake Valley that are more dramatic than anything you might expect. Once past the bridge, bear right and get ready to start climbing in earnest.

8.7 The East Fork of the Rattlesnake enters here, as does Trail 514; a sign on the right indicates 4 miles to Mineral Peak and 5 miles to Sheep Mountain (see Ride 20).

9.0 A viewpoint offers a grand view of the valley and creek-carved rocks below. Snow can be seen on nearby mountaintops through much of the year. At this point the road changes character a little; plants become more plentiful atop the center ridge, and the path itself alternates between packed dirt and loose rocks.

10.5 Trail descends for a mile or more.

13.1 Cross wooden bridge over Porcupine Creek, an alder-choked tributary of Rattlesnake Creek.

13.5 Pass Porcupine Creek on right; in a small clearing you'll find a sign for Porcupine Creek Trail 504. Continue climbing main road.

14.2 Negotiate a brief descent, eventually coming upon Wrangle Bridge.

14.9 Reach Wrangle Bridge, just below the wilderness boundary.

15.0 T-stop marks the end of the road for bicycles. It is illegal to take them into the wilderness! Some combine hiking and biking, stashing their bikes here, but remember that respecting the law is the key to maintaining access. The trail on your right, heading north, is Wrangle Creek Trail 502; on your left is Lake Creek Trail 534. Return the way you came.

Wallman Trail–
Spring Gulch Loop

Location: Rattlesnake National Recreation Area north of downtown.

Distance: 8.3-mile loop.

Time: 1 hour.

Tread: Singletrack.

Aerobic level: Very strenuous.

Technical difficulty: Level 4.

Highlights: This steep, technical trail carries from the heart of the Rattlesnake Valley into some close-to-home heights through fields of wildflowers, while offering one of the more challenging short rides in the area. Recently reworked by the Forest Service and volunteers from LIMB and IMBA, the intent seems to be to offer an alternative to many of the more popular rides in the Rattlesnake. Still, only the truly talented and strongest riders will be able to climb this route in either direction without taking a break. The reward? Screaming, generally unpopulated down-hilling.

Land status: The entire loop is on national forest land within the Rattlesnake National Recreation Area.

Maps: USGS Northeast Missoula and Lolo National Forest. A permanent map of the entire Rattlesnake National Recreation and Wilderness Area is installed at the trailhead and

•Wallman Trail–Spring Gulch Loop

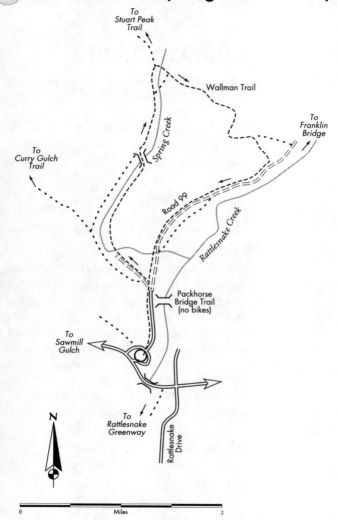

To Stuart Peak
Trail

Wallman Trail

To
Franklin
Bridge

To
Curry Gulch
Trail

Spring Creek

Road 99

Rattlesnake Creek

Packhorse
Bridge Trail
(no bikes)

To
Sawmill
Gulch

N

To
Rattlesnake
Greenway

Rattlesnake Drive

0   Miles   2

maps of the Sawmill-Curry Trail System (available at the trailhead and Forest Service Region 1 Headquarters) show the Spring Gulch section of the ride.

Access: Driving, follow Van Buren Avenue to Rattlesnake Drive from East Broadway, or take the Van Buren exit off I–90 and head north. You can also ride the Rattlesnake Greenway from downtown (see Ride 11 for directions). Take a right after 2.5 miles, staying on Rattlesnake Drive, and then a left after about 4 miles once the drive starts to snake through the woods. Here you will see a sign for the Rattlesnake Main trailhead; follow the road over the bridge that straddles Rattlesnake Creek and bear right to the main parking lot.

The Ride

0.0 Park at main trailhead to Rattlesnake National Recreation Area. A permanent map and sign board are just beyond the gated entrance heading up the gravel road, Road 99, which parallels the creek. After 0.25 mile, beyond an old jeep trail on left (see Ride 3), this trail skirts a rock wall on your left. Watch for pedestrians, and keep under the posted speed limit!

0.4 The valley opens up. The pack bridge from the horse trailhead will be on the right; a sign on the left indicates mileage and various trails. Follow signs

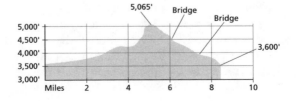

for Franklin Bridge and wilderness boundary along Road 99.

0.6 Singletrack spurs appear in succession on the right and left. To avoid user conflict, stay on main road, which climbs gradually and enters the woods.

0.8 Pass another singletrack spur and outhouse on the right as you bear left on Road 99.

2.0 See sign for Wallman Trail and Spring Gulch on left. Turn here (a second turnoff will be on your left 0.5 mile farther down the road).

2.2 Take left at fork in trail.

2.6 A steep, technical section climbs for 0.1 mile, tops above gully, and then carries down to hook up with second Wallman Trail access and start of the challenging climb.

2.7 Take left onto Wallman Trail; start climbing in earnest.

2.8 Insurmountable singletrack lies straight ahead; take left up a more gradual slope.

2.9 A sharp elbow bears right as a view opens to the valley you traveled through to get here, marked by evergreen forest and the meandering Rattlesnake Creek. For the next 0.25 mile, the trail gets steeper from here.

3.2 A faint trail appears on the left, cutting across the hill face. Stay to your right on well-worn singletrack.

3.7 Reach first switchback; trail turns to soft dirt as you snake uphill.

4.0 After a brief descent through a spring gully, the trail climbs once again. I had to walk my bike here.

4.3 Congratulations! You've endured the most challenging section of the ride. Continue straight ahead on the right fork of the trail until you reach a second fork. On your right now, the trail heads uphill to Stuart Peak. Take a left here, dropping over a steep, technical descent into Spring Creek drainage. Obstacles include roots, wooden and rubber water bars, and a few culverts.

4.8   Trail enters Spring Creek drainage. The valley opens up, and you can finally get your head up to enjoy the creek and wildflowers. Bear left.

4.9   Continue moderately gradual descent, finding a massive downed tree across the trail.

5.1   Watch for extreme drop as you reach headwaters of Spring Creek, which you'll cross, bearing left.

5.2   Continue descending; culverts are the main obstacles here. Watch for other users!

5.7   Trail branches, with right headed up Curry Gulch to Sawmill Gulch (see Ride 3). Take a left, either crossing the creek on the wooden bridge or simply riding through the water on the trail below. Continue descent as singletrack widens eventually to an old dirt road as it nears the main basin.

7.0   Forest Service outhouse is on the right as other trails enter the route. Watch for foot traffic!

7.5   MOUNTAIN BIKERS ALERT sign lays out trail etiquette as the trail flattens out and returns to the Rattlesnake drainage and mouth of the recreation area.

7.6   The trail reaches Road 99; once again, take a right toward the main trailhead. Note the posted speed limit!

7.7   Cross Spring Creek on bridge, installed in 1999 in response to flood conditions following record snows the winter of 1997–1998.

7.8   Pass pack bridge and signs for additional trails.

8.1   Jeep track from upper Rattlesnake parking area enters on right; continue straight toward permanent maps and main parking lot.

8.3   Return to main trailhead/parking—ride done.

Mount Jumbo–
Woods Gulch Loop

Location: The hills on the northeast edge of Missoula.

Distance: 7.1-mile loop.

Time: 1 hour, 10 minutes.

Tread: Singletrack, doubletrack, and small amount on dirt and paved roads.

Aerobic level: Very strenuous.

Technical difficulty: Level 4.

Highlights: This loop connects to a variety of other Missoula trails, while offering high views from the saddle of Mount Jumbo and a swell, tricky downhill through Woods Gulch. Mount Jumbo, a cornerstone of the Missoula open-space plan, is closed part of the year to help the elk herd that winters on the mountain, but in other seasons abundant wildlife can be found hereabouts.

Land status: Missoula Open Space, State of Montana, and Lolo National Forest.

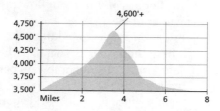

•Mount Jumbo–Woods Gulch Loop

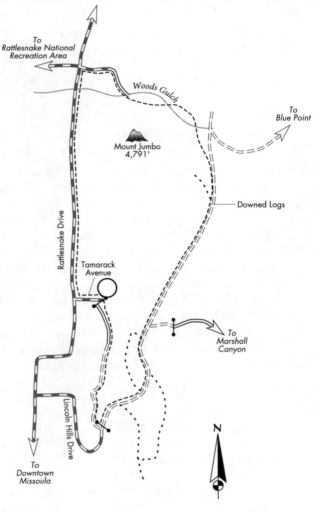

To
Rattlesnake National
Recreation Area

Woods Gulch

To
Blue Point

Mount Jumbo
4,791'

Downed Logs

Rattlesnake Drive

Tamarack
Avenue

To
Marshall
Canyon

Lincoln Hills Drive

To
Downtown
Missoula

N

0   Miles   2

Maps: USGS Northeast Missoula and Lolo National Forest. Permanent maps are posted at the gates at the head of Tamarack Avenue and the hilltop entry to Mount Jumbo.

Access: By car, from downtown Missoula, head north along Van Buren Avenue toward the Rattlesnake National Recreation Area, bearing right nearly 2 miles out onto Tamarack Avenue, where parking can be found at the trailhead. Bikes can follow the same route.

The Ride

0.0 From the east end of Tamarack Avenue, head south through the gate and climb the dirt road (closed year-round to motorized vehicles).

0.1 Reach minor plateau, bearing right then left on road as you keep climbing. A singletrack path parallels the fence above. Shortly you reach a second fence with a private sheep and llama pasture just downhill to the right.

0.3 Continue climbing, as views of the Missoula and Bitterroot Valleys open up to the south.

0.7 Take the sharp left turn up to the access for Mount Jumbo, riding around the fence and continuing up the dirt road as it degrades from jeep track to doubletrack.

0.8 As you reach the upcoming fork, bear right onto the North Loop Trail.

1.3 An overgrown ranch road branches off; take your first right, following the ridgeline trail. Ignore the trail that parallels the power lines and stay straight, heading for the upper saddle.

1.7 Reach a hilltop plateau with views of upper Clark Fork River Valley, the Sapphire Mountains, and

Missoula's eastern suburbs below. At the upcoming fork, take a left, heading immediately uphill for the most challenging approach to the top of Woods Gulch. A right will carry you around to a more gradual slope and the Marshall Grade (see Ride 1). As you climb, the doubletrack becomes increasingly rutted, while the tall pines create some shade from the elements.

2.6 A vague trail departs, heading down to the left; continue straight. A tree crosses the trail ahead, forcing you to follow the trail around it to the right—unless you have serious skills that will allow you to use the branches laid down to hop over the tree. Doubletrack turns to singletrack.

2.8 The trail forks; take right and keep climbing.

3.4 The trail levels out as you reach the top of this section and approach the Woods Gulch drop-off.

3.7 Trail intersects with Woods Gulch, a singletrack entering from the downhill left. (Continuing straight gets you to a road in just over 0.25 mile, one of the approaches to Blue Point and Sheep Mountain; see Ride 20.) Take this left, and begin descending the challenging downhill of Woods Gulch.

4.2 The trail gets increasingly rocky as it descends, eventually overlapping a stream, which it crosses in a jumble of loose rock another 0.5 mile onward.

4.7 Cross a stream and continue descent. Watch for pedestrians!

5.0 As you approach the gulch bottom, the trail enters into the elbow of a road that bends around to the right. Stay your course, descending on a gravel road. Look out for vehicle traffic and loose gravel!

5.5 The gravel turns to pavement as the hill bottoms out alongside a few homes in the Rattlesnake Valley.

5.7 Reach Rattlesnake Drive. You are pretty much directly across from the Rattlesnake National Recreation Area's main trailhead and a variety of other rides. Take a left here, heading south, back toward Tamarack Avenue and downtown.

6.9 Take a left onto Tamarack Avenue to return to your starting point (or continue toward town).

7.1 Return to gate at east end of Tamarack Avenue.

Garnet Ghost Town–Summit Cabin Loop

Location: The Garnet Mountains, 30 miles east of Missoula.

Distance: 9.8-mile loop.

Time: 1 hour, 15 minutes.

Tread: Well-maintained dirt roads.

Aerobic level: Strenuous.

Technical difficulty: Level 2.

Highlights: This ride might draw cries of derision from those seeking a gnarly, singletrack experience, but the roads followed here travel through some dynamite high country

•Garnet Ghost Town–Summit Cabin Loop

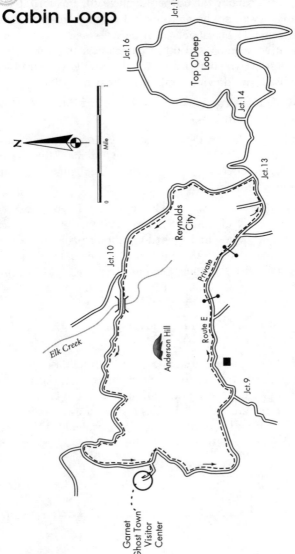

and offer a glimpse at Montana's mining past. The pine and aspen woods along the Garnet Range Road, a national back-country byway, are home to many creatures, and the many joined circuits hereabouts provide awesome views of the Mission Mountains and other ranges near and far. If you come this far, you'll also want to take a walking tour of the town itself, just down the hill from the parking lot.

Land status: A combination of private and Bureau of Land Management property.

Maps: USGS Union Peak, USGS Elevation Mountain, and Lolo National Forest (west half). Free trail maps for cyclists and snowmobilers are available at the small shop in what's left of downtown Garnet.

Access: The fastest way to Garnet Ghost Town is to head out from Missoula along Highway 200 for 22 miles; then take a right, following signs along the dirt road to Garnet Ghost Town, about 14 miles in. The town may also be reached by driving about 35 miles on I–90 and heading north 10 miles after taking the Bearmouth exit.

The Ride

0.0   Leave parking lot; take a left for brief descent.

0.2   Take a left again, climbing now, keeping an eye open for the marker for Junction 5. (These junctions are part of the designated snowmobile trails and can be found on the maps available at the Garnet Ghost Town store.) Climb briefly.

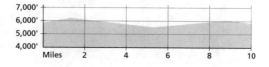

0.3 Take a sharp right toward I–90 (as indicated on signpost) and climb some more.

0.4 As you round the bend, bearing left, there's a sign for Anderson Hill, a hill you will circumnavigate during this ride. Keep on the main road, bearing right at the fork.

0.9 A gully lies directly in front; keep to road.

1.4 At gated mine site on left, continue on road, which descends briefly. Keep an eye out for Junction 9.

1.9 At Junction 9, which also bears markers for Routes E and H, take a left, following Route E uphill.

2.1 A demolished shack can be found on the right, downhill side of the road just before the upcoming fork. Bear left again, and keep climbing. (The road to the right actually forms a little roundabout that reconnects with Route E.)

2.2 Roundabout enters from right, and old mine tailing is visible uphill to the left. Shortly a rutted jeep trail veers to the right; continue climbing on main road.

2.5 Reach another fork in the road as this hill tops out; follow the orange arrows around to the right and begin descent.

2.8 Pass slash from a logging operation on right; stay on the main road and continue descent.

3.3 Enter private property; stay on road as you pass through open gate. Take care to stay on the road, as old mining tunnels have collapsed nearby. You'll pass an orange "pond" marking one such failure within a couple hundred yards on your right—a reminder of history.

3.7 On your left, a clearing in the trees offers views.

3.9 Exit private land through second gate; keep descending. Additional roads enter from the right and then the left over the next 0.75 mile. Stay on the main, obvious road, still Route E.

4.8 Take a left at the fork.

4.9 Reach Junction 13, which hooks up with Route B and the Top O' Deep Loop. Here you can look down into the Elk Creek drainage, admire the flora and occasional fauna, and enjoy views of the Garnet Mountains.

5.9 Take the sharp left on the road entering from the downhill right.

6.0 Remnants of a community known as Reynolds City can be found in the clearing on left.

6.5 Cross cattle guard.

6.8 At Junction 10 take a left, following signs for Garnet Range Road and Highway 200.

7.1 Cross Elk Creek on bridge and begin climbing. An old mining road enters from the left, while the view to the right offers an outstanding panorama of the backside of the Mission Mountains.

7.7 The Elk Creek overlook to your right offers a view of Elevation Mountain—the highest peak in the Garnet Range—across the drainage; an interpretive sign explains about wildlife and land use in this area. Keep climbing.

9.0 Take a left at the fork, and climb around the bend, leaving behind the Garnet Range Road as you return to the complex of roads around the ghost town.

9.3 An old mining road comes in from the left. Shortly you pass a sign that marks the area as a NO SHOOTING zone.

9.5 Take a left at T-stop, descending toward the town of Garnet.

9.6 Take a right at Junction 5, returning to parking lot above.

9.8 Reach parking lot.

Lake Como Loop

Location: Bitterroot Valley south of Missoula, 5 miles northwest of the small town of Darby.

Distance: 8-mile loop.

Time: 1–1.5 hours.

Tread: Singletrack.

Aerobic level: Moderate.

Technical difficulty: Level 3+.

Highlights: This popular recreation trail, circumnavigating a man-made lake built in 1905, follows a relatively flat but still challenging course along the shore. For those used to the ups-and-downs of most area trails, this provides a flatter track that can be tackled with relative ease. Exposed rock outcroppings at the far end of the lake and a couple of sandy pits provide technical challenges, as do a couple of steep stream crossings. The path itself has a wider range of surfaces than most tracks discussed in this book. Intermediate riders will appreciate the chance to work on skills; for more advanced riders, two laps would make an excellent workout. Camping is available.

Land status: Lolo National Forest. (The dam itself is under the Bureau of Reclamation's jurisdiction.)

Maps: USGS Darby, and USGS Como Peaks, and Bitterroot National Forest.

•Lake Como Loop

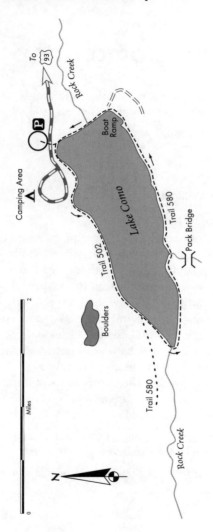

Access: Take Highway 93 south from Missoula into the Bitterroot Valley. Lake Como is located off Lake Como Road, which parallels Rock Creek heading west out of Darby. Follow signs to Lake Como, about ninety minutes south of Missoula. Park at the trailhead.

Note: This destination is part of the federal Fee Demonstration Project and requires a recreation pass, available in Darby at the Darby Ranger Station off Highway 93.

The Ride

0.0   Leave the parking lot on the north side of the dam, pedaling west along a paved trail with benches and interpretive signs. Area rules and a map are at the trailhead.

0.4   Pavement ends; the trail turns to smooth dirt singletrack.

0.7   Dirt gives way to a rocky section with loose stones and roots, continuing for about 1 mile.

1.5   The trail begins a gentle decent. Vegetation increases along the path.

2.0   The trail cuts between boulders and trees, including an impressive spruce, passing a sandy area on the left. Expect more technical challenges as you move beyond the flat section here.

2.2   Cross stream, take a quick left, and begin short moderate decent.

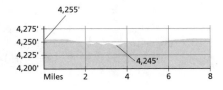

2.6   Skirt huge rocks, climbing briefly up a slightly technical ascent before descending once again.

2.9   Cross a second, larger creek. Then climb very briefly, shortly pedaling past a few truly impressive boulders on the order of 20- to 30-feet tall.

3.1   The trail comes to a intersection with Rock Creek Trail 580 (which heads uphill to your right). Keep to the left, following the sign for Lake Como Loop Trail and entering a more technical section where trail improvement efforts include wooden water bars. Exposed rock and sandy soil alternate until the upcoming bridge.

3.2   A small bridge carries you over another creek, which is followed by a challenging climb over natural stone steps. The trail bends sharply to the right, traversing more exposed bedrock. Continue around the far end of the lake. Be prepared for plenty of obstacles.

3.6   Encounter a short, rocky climb with additional wooden water bars across the trail. Loose dirt and rock follows for nearly 0.5 mile. This side of the lake is open to horses as well, so keep a look out for riders.

4.2   Cross two rocky streambeds. If it's wet and water's running, cross on the pack bridges 10 yards upstream to the right.

5.5   The trail flattens as it turns to sandy, well-packed soil. Riding through the trees, begin the gradual climb along the south shoreline.

7.2   The boat ramp should come into view on your left. Bear right at the fork in the trail; directly across the road, a white sign marks the trail. Bear right again, heading into the trees above the boat ramp.

7.3   The trail reaches the top of the dam. Ride around the cement wall and interpretive sign; ride across the dam.

7.8 Reach the far shore and the end of the dam. Continue straight, crossing the bridge, and take a left on the pavement. Shortly the pavement turns to gravel. Follow the signs back to the day-use and parking area.

8.0 Parking lot will be on left; ride over.

Blodgett Canyon

Location: South of Missoula in the Bitterroot Valley, past Hamilton near the Idaho border.

Distance: 14 miles round-trip.

Time: 3 hours.

Tread: Singletrack.

Aerobic level: Strenuous.

Technical difficulty: Level 4-5+.

Highlights: When I was first informed that folks tackle this popular, scenic hiking trail on their bikes, I was in disbelief. Despite having been burned by the massive forest fires of 2000, the trail offers glimpses of high cliff walls (often enjoyed by rock climbers) and follows the route of a classic Bitterroot trout stream (enjoyed by anglers). After the first couple of miles, however, the trail gets so technical that only the most skilled riders will want to try. Beyond the pack bridge nearly 4 miles in—an excellent turnaround

•Blodgett Canyon

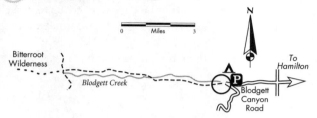

point for you mortals—the trail leads to the wilderness boundary at 7 miles (bikes prohibited beyond this point). The boulder-strewn trail offers the most technical riding that I tackled in the course of riding for this book. There are riders who will enjoy the sheer challenge of this trail, especially those with full-suspension who find the other rides herein too wimpy. The rest of you have been warned.

Land status: National Forest.

Maps: USGS Hamilton North, USGS Printz Ridge, and Bitterroot National Forest.

Access: Head south on Highway 93 to Hamilton. Take a right onto Bowman and then a left onto Ricketts Road. Follow this road to a sharp right turn onto Blodgett Canyon Road. After a couple of miles, the parking lot and primitive campground at the road's end, where you'll find the trailhead.

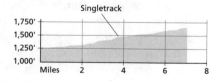

The Ride

0.0 Start in the campground parking lot. Ride across the bridge you drove across, and take an immediate right onto the singletrack. The first section is tight and twisty—and brutally rocky.

0.2 The singletrack merges with a pack trail. The billboard just off the trail has rules, closure warnings, and a map of the area.

0.3 Pass the Don Mackey memorial sculpture. For the next mile, things are pretty treacherous as the rocky trail twists through the trees. Keep an eye out for other trail users.

1.3 Enter a boulder-strewn area where the trees have been eliminated by avalanches, and the trail continues its rocky way. Up to your right catch the first view of the awesome cliffs along the north wall of the valley.

1.5 Near Blodgett Creek, with its beautiful pools. The trail briefly smoothes out as you cross soil and duff, then becomes increasingly rough to ride over the next 0.25 mile.

1.7 The canopy opens up. Boulders on the trail make for tough going. The cliffs above are spectacular, but good luck taking your eyes off the trail for the next 1.5 miles.

3.7 Reach a pack bridge over the creek. Cross and take a left, continuing upstream. Stay on the main stem, and avoid game trails and angler paths that run to the creek. For the next mile, things get a little easier.

4.7 The canyon narrows; the trail gets steeper. You'll plateau shortly on an embankment that overlooks the creek and a small waterfall.

5.0 If you've made it this far, you'll be surprised to find that the trail gets harder yet. A series of technical climbs over the next half mile or so will challenge even the most proficient riders. But then, remarkably, the trail gets a little easier. The next 2 miles will test the toughest riders, alternating between more technical nastiness and a few easier sections.

7.0 Reach the wilderness boundary. Another mile ahead is Blodgett Lake, but you cannot take your bike into the wilderness. Stow it in the woods if you want to swim, or turn back and try to enjoy the decent. Coming out is much more fun than going in!

Rattlesnake Greenway

Location: North of downtown Missoula and the Rattlesnake neighborhood, leading to the Rattlesnake National Recreation Area.

Distance: 1.4 miles one-way.

Time: 10–15 minutes.

Tread: Singletrack and doubletrack.

Aerobic level: Easy.

Technical difficulty: Level 2.

Highlights: This sweet little section of trail running north-south along Rattlesnake Creek is primarily a route to travel

•Rattlesnake Greenway

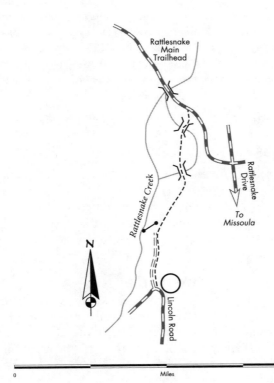

Rattlesnake Main Trailhead

Rattlesnake Creek

N

Rattlesnake Drive

To Missoula

Lincoln Road

0   Miles   2

Bridge

Bridge

3,600'
3,500'
3,400'

Miles   1   2

from town to the Rattlesnake National Recreation Area. It's a generally smooth track, with a few small obstacles, popular with pedestrians as well as cyclists. Great for beginners and adequate for working on skills and getting warmed up for longer rides, the greenway rolls through ponderosa pines and picturesque clearings, generally sticking close to the creek, and provides an alternative to the paved routes leading to the recreation area. A web of singletrack throughout the park also provides a nice practice zone.

Land status: City of Missoula, and private property easements.

Maps: USGS Northeast Missoula.

Access: At the north end of the Lincolnwood subdivision, you'll find a parking area near the park. This trail can also be reached by backtracking from the Rattlesnake National Recreation Area parking lot, heading up the road toward Rattlesnake Drive and taking a right through the trees.

The Ride

0.0 The greenway starts immediately north of the wooden fence. A wide, red dirt path heads into the trees; singletrack loops cut through the trees on the left.

0.1 Enter the woods, riding through wide-spaced ponderosa pines with Rattlesnake Creek on your left.

0.3 A bridge crosses a tributary to the creek, followed by a short climb.

0.4 Spot RATTLESNAKE TRAIL TO RECREATION AREA sign with a little schematic map and reminders that you are crossing private property. Veer uphill to the right.

0.5 Cross ranch road. Follow the fenceline, which carries you through trees and brush and then over a bridge crossing an irrigation ditch. There's a pasture on the right (usually with horses in it) and brush on your left. Continue straight ahead along the fence.

0.8 Reenter the trees. Stay on left-hand path, around the bend to your right. Be careful not to run off the trail! Just a couple of rotations will get you to the top of this quick hill; then pick one of the jeep treads paralleling the fence.

1.0 The trail gets rocky then a little more interesting just beyond the ATTENTION BICYCLISTS! sign and the clearing. Descend ever so briefly, then enter woods where minor obstacles—rocks, roots, and a well-worn gully (which is sometimes bridged by a board)—should provide a bit of fun.

1.2 Bridge up ahead—slippery when wet! Cross over the creek and stay to your right.

1.4 Coming out of the woods, you'll find the road to the Rattlesnake National Recreation Area trailhead. A left on the pavement will carry you downhill, over the creek and to the parking area. A right takes you to Rattlesnake Drive.

Clark Fork
Riverfront Trail

Location: Downtown.

Distance: 1.9 miles one-way.

Time: 10–15 minutes.

Tread: Gravel road (nonmotorized traffic only).

Aerobic level: Easy.

Technical difficulty: Level 1.

Highlights: Largely a commuter track and running path, this downtown riverfront trail passes through several appealing parks on the south side of the Clark Fork River. Good for families and for accessing trails east of town, it's a fast trail, wide and flat, which provides a practice surface for individuals new to the sport and for others when snow lingers in the high country. Cyclists will want to watch for pedestrians and dog walkers.

Land status: City of Missoula.

Maps: USGS Southwest Missoula and USGS Southeast Missoula.

Access: Spanning several parks, this urban trail through the heart of Missoula can be accessed at Hickory Street on its west end a block west of the main thoroughfare of Orange Street. Orange Street runs north-south 2 blocks east of Chestnut Street. It runs beneath the Higgins Avenue

•Clark Fork Riverfront Trail

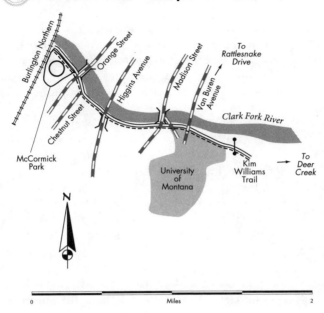

Bridge, continues east past the University of Montana, and connects to the Kim Williams Trail at the base of Mount Sentinel just before Hellgate Canyon. I've described it here traveling west to east.

The Ride

0.0 Enter McCormick Park, passing a pond on your left and tennis courts on your right. Head toward the river, then bear right as you reach the river. The train trestle will be on your left.

0.3 You'll ride beneath the Orange Street Bridge, entering Clark Fork Natural Park. The wide singletrack spur immediately to the right after the bridge connects to the Chestnut Street entrance to the park and an upper trail that parallels the one you're on.

0.5 The path bends to the right, following the irrigation slough, and crosses a footbridge, meeting up with the parallel path from Chestnut Street. Bear left at this intersection.

0.7 As you near the Clark Fork once again, bear right on the trail, passing the Old Milwaukee Station. Cross under the Higgins Avenue Bridge and shortly enter John Toole Riverfront Park.

0.9 Past the high school football practice fields, there are public rest rooms to your right. Another access point to the park is available here as the west end of Fourth Avenue merges with the park.

1.2 Pass under the Jefferson Street Bridge and pass over a creek.

1.3 The University of Montana practice field should be on your right. After another 0.1 mile the university footbridge, crossing the river to the north, will be on your left.

1.7 Just after the gated university security compound on your right, see a small sign for the footpath up Mount Sentinel.

1.9 Reach the signed gate that marks the entrance of the Kim Williams Natural Area, which runs through Hellgate Canyon and connects to the Deer Creek–Pattee Canyon Loop (see Ride 2).

Lumberjack Loop

Location: Off Highway 12 southwest of Missoula and near the Idaho border.

Distance: 27.2-mile loop.

Time: 2–3 hours.

Tread: Primarily dirt and gravel logging roads with a short section of paved highway early on.

Aerobic level: Strenuous.

Technical difficulty: Level 1–2.

Highlights: This is a challenging alternative to some of the technical rides in this volume. The ride, an isolated loop along logging roads through the Bitterroot Mountains, begins and ends at the legendary Lumberjack Tavern, a ramshackle old bar with giant logs cut into bar stools and an enormous stone fireplace. Breaks in the forest along the ridgelines allow views of the peaks of the Bitterroot Range at various points, and the country is home to a variety of wildlife. Signs of continued logging remind us that the paraphernalia decorating the Lumberjack Tavern was in use until recently. The loop features a couple of tough climbs and is long enough to make a great training ride for those looking to log miles as well as build technical expertise.

Land status: Clearwater National Forest, and Plum Creek Timer Company.

Maps: USGS Lupine Creek, USGS Deer Park, USGS Petty Mountain, and Lolo National Forest (west half).

⊙•Lumberjack Loop

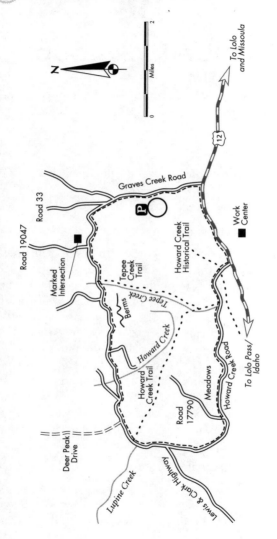

Access: From Missoula, head south on Highway 93 for 11 miles; take a right on Highway 12, heading west from the bedroom community of Lolo. Continue 16 miles, and take the right at Graves Creek Road 489. Continue heading north along this road until you get to the Lumberjack Tavern, where you can park and maybe grab a cold drink when you finish the loop.

The Ride

0.0 Starting from the parking lot at the Lumberjack Tavern, take a right, heading back toward Highway 12.

0.4 A creek passes under the road. You'll see a driveway doubling back to your right; continue until you reach Highway 12.

1.5 Reach Highway 12; take a right, heading west parallel to Lolo Creek on the other side of the road. Climb for 2+ miles—watch for traffic, especially big rigs heading for the pass into Idaho!

3.8 Just after you pass the work center on your left, take a right onto Howard Creek Road 238, heading north again.

3.9 As you start up Howard Creek, there is an entrance for Howard Creek Historical Trail, a footpath where

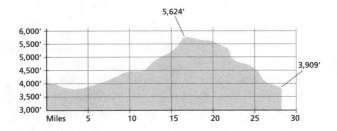

there is an interpretive sign and public rest rooms. Continue on the road.

4.5 Intersect with the North Fork Howard Creek Trail, which branches off to the right, rising steeply. Continue on Road 238, climbing gradually.

5.1 Keep going straight, past logging road to your right.

6.2 Pass an additional logging road. Stay on Road 238, keeping straight for the next 5 miles and passing through a small valley where you'll spot the road up Teepee Creek to your right. Shortly there is a small, seasonal pond on your left.

11.3 Road 17790 enters from the right as you bear left around a long curve. The ascent begins to increase as Road 238 winds uphill.

12.1 At this plateau you'll reach the junction with Howard Creek Trail 204 and the Lewis and Clark Highway. Take a sharp right on Road 238, and keep on climbing. Views of the Bitterroot and Clearwater National Forests open up to your left immediately. More mountain vistas can be found a couple of miles up the road on your right.

14.1 From the left, an overgrown jeep track enters the road. Descend on the road.

15.2 Reach the intersection of Howard and Lupine Creeks. Additional logging roads run into Road 238 at miles 15.5, 16, 16.2 (gated), and 16.3. Keep going straight, and be prepared for serious climbing.

16.6 Enjoy views south all the way to the Selway Wilderness Area from this ridge to your right, and you can see where Highway 12 and Lolo Creek cut the valley below. The trail begins to flatten out shortly.

17.6 Tepee Ridge Trail enters from the right. From here, if you were up for the challenge, you could descend back to Howard Creek over some steep and gnarly terrain. Continue on Road 238 to complete Lumberjack Loop.

18.0 Road enters from the right; stay straight.

18.6 Additional logging roads intersect with Road 238. A jeep track heads up the knob. Stay left on Road 238, passing gated areas and more roads until you come to the marked intersection with Road 19047 after a little more than a mile.

20.0 Begin your descent on Wagon Mountain Road 33. Have fun!

22.7 Another road enters from right; stay straight and keep descending.

24.2 Road 33 meets up with a creek drainage, which parallels a road merging from the left. Take a right.

24.6 Continue descent as you pass the intersection with Graves Creek Road, a gated logging road, and signs indicating mileage to North Fork Howard Creek Trail and Fish Creek Road. (The one-way climb over the mountains from Fish Creek to the Lumberjack Tavern is another popular area ride.) The forest opens up into meadows as you reach the bottom of the hill.

25.6 Keep straight as you pass roads entering from the right and left in succession.

27.0 Through the trees you should be able to see the Lumberjack Tavern ahead.

27.2 Return to parking lot.

Crazy Creek–
Mount Sentinel Peak

Location: Mount Sentinel on the eastern edge of Missoula, accessed from Pattee Canyon.

Distance: 3.5 miles one-way to the top; 7 miles round-trip.

Time: 30–45 minutes up; 15–20 minutes down.

Tread: Mixed single- and doubletrack with some sections of dirt road and jeep track in various stages of deterioration.

Aerobic level: Strenuous.

Technical difficulty: Level 4–5+ with at least one portion most everyone will have to walk.

Highlights: This can be done as part of a day or an afternoon exploring Pattee Canyon (see Rides 2 and 4) or as a single short, technical climb with rewarding views. The scene from the top of Mount Sentinel is amazing, providing glimpses of all the five valleys surrounding Missoula and an almost bird's-eye view of the town itself. Surprisingly, given the popularity of the area for hikers and bikers, the summit of Mount Sentinel doesn't really see that many visitors— but that's testimony to the challenge of this trail.

Land status: Lolo National Forest and State of Montana.

Maps: USGS Northeast Missoula and Lolo National Forest. The Forest Service Region 1 Headquarters also produces a trail guide for the Pattee Canyon Recreation Area.

•Crazy Creek–
Mount Sentinel Peak

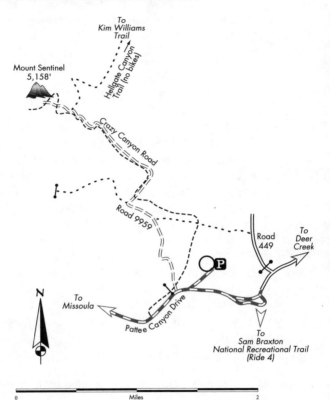

Mount Sentinel
5,158'

To
Kim Williams
Trail

Hellgate Canyon
Trail (no bikes)

Crazy Canyon Road

Road 9959

Road
449

To
Deer
Creek

P

N

To
Missoula

Pattee Canyon Drive

To
Sam Braxton
National Recreational Trail
(Ride 4)

0   Miles   2

5,158'

5,000'
4,500'
4,000'
3,500'

Miles   1   2   3   4

Access: From downtown Missoula take Higgins Avenue south to the junction with Pattee Canyon Drive, just past the University Golf Course on your left. Riding the pavement up Pattee Canyon Drive is another option, following the road, which is also the course for the annual Pattee Canyon Hill Climb each fall. If you drive, park in the Pattee Canyon Recreational Area lots.

The Ride

0.0 From the parking lot follow the fenceline about a 0.5 mile downhill on Pattee Canyon Road to the Crazy Creek trailhead. Maps to the Pattee Canyon Recreation Area are available here.

0.4 Take a right onto the wide, rocky singletrack, and start climbing, crossing Crazy Canyon Road 9959. A sign indicates that the Hellgate Canyon trailhead (closed to bicycles) is 3 miles away and Mount Sentinel is 3.5 miles. Stay on the main trail.

0.5 Reach a clearing in the trees, pass a picnic area, and cross Road 9959 again, hopping the big dirt berm on the opposite side; stick to the singletrack. (Road 9959 will get you to the top, but the singletrack is more fun.)

1.5 The singletrack merges with Road 9959 once again. This time, take a right, heading up the road. Taking the singletrack across at this point leads to a dead end.

2.1 Leave Lolo National Forest and enter state land. Stay on the main path.

3.0 Arrive at ridgeline; note orange gate. Here the road intersects with Hellgate Canyon Trail 11—no bikes allowed! Take the singletrack along the ridge from here on out. The road disintegrates well before the peak. You'll encounter some fairly steep switch-backs, ride across roots and wooden water bars, and cross the rutted remains of the road a couple of times.

3.5 As you emerge on the bald knob that caps Mount Sentinel, the trail and road run together once again. Enjoy the panorama before heading back the way you came.

Blue Mountain Lookout–Deadman Ridge

Location: Blue Mountain Recreation Area, 2 miles south-west of Missoula.

Distance: 22.2-mile loop.

Time: 2–3 hours up; 1–3 hours down; 3–6 hours round-trip.

Tread: 14 miles on gravel and primitive roads and 8.2 miles of singletrack.

Aerobic level: Moderately strenuous–strenuous.

Technical difficulty: Level 1–2 on the way up; 3–4+ on the way down.

•Blue Mountain Lookout–
Deadman Ridge

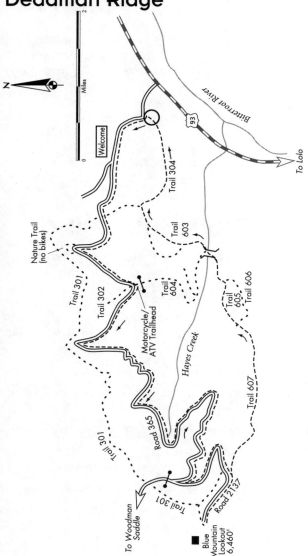

Highlights: The system of trails at the Blue Mountain National Recreation Area is one of the first to dry out after the winter and provides a wide variety of options for beginners as well as expert mountain bikers. This ride involves a long, nontechnical climb to yet another peak that is hard by Missoula standards. The recreation area is home to many species of animals and a nice variety of plant life—although exotic weeds have taken over sections of the landscape. Cars are allowed on most of the road portion of this ride, and during the summer it gets mighty dusty. Still, Blue Mountain provides a good place to build stamina and get familiar with handling techniques. As of this writing, the sweet singletrack of Deadman Ridge, which I've included as a route for descent, had not gained the popularity of similar trails found in the Rattlesnake National Recreation Area, perhaps due to the relative challenges of tackling the steep and technical terrain it offers. Ultimately, only truly hardy riders will want to try to climb Blue Mountain via the ridge, but intermediates and experts alike will enjoy the challenge of the thrilling Deadman downhill.

Land status: Lolo National Forest

Maps: USGS Southwest Missoula and USGS Blue Mountain. The Forest Service also has recreation area maps available at the trailhead.

Access: From Missoula travel 2 miles south of Reserve Street on Highway 93; turn right on Blue Mountain Road (County Road 30). Stay on Blue Mountain Road for 0.5 mile, where you'll find the trailhead for the National Recreational Trail (bikes are prohibited), Trail 304 (bikes are allowed—a good thing because this forms the outrun from Deadman Gulch), and horse-loading facilities. This is the best place to park if you plan to come down Deadman Gulch; it's also where this ride description begins.

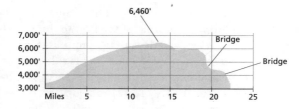

You can also continue about another 0.25 mile on Blue Mountain Road, bearing left at Road 365, which leads to the main entrance to the recreation area and additional parking areas.

The Ride

0.0 Starting from the main trailhead for the Blue Mountain National Recreation Trail and horse-loading area, take a left, heading west on the gravel-surfaced Blue Mountain Road.

0.7 Bear left at the intersection, leaving Blue Mountain Road and picking up Road 365. Cross a cattle guard and head toward a large WELCOME sign, where you will find area maps. (Trail 308, across the way, connects to a network of trails—including many biking opportunities—on the face of Blue Mountain.) Start your gradual ascent.

0.9 The weird yellow basket just off the road on your right is Hole 9 of the Blue Mountain Folf Course (disc golf).

1.2 Trail 309 enters the road on your left. Parking is available on the right (not a bad place to park if you plan on skipping Deadman Gulch). The fenced-in area just up the hill is a knapweed research plot. Continue on Road 365.

1.5 Trail 301 (pedestrians and horses only—no bikes) intersects with Road 365. More parking is available just ahead; stay on Road 365.

2.1 Follow Road 365 as it veers left around the bend. Keep climbing.

2.5 Pass the Blue Mountain Nature Trail 401. No bikes!

3.6 Trail 304 on your left provides a route to descend back toward the main trailhead and horse-loading area. Uphill to your right, Trail 302 (pedestrians and horses only—no bikes) heads uphill. Through the gate at the next bend, you can enter the motorcycle/ATV access, where biking is allowed. Continue on Road 365 as it weaves up the mountain to get to the lookout on the road.

4.1 Pass a gate; continue climbing.

4.4 A fence parallels the road to your left. This is a good rest area, affording a view of Missoula's south hills across the valley floor.

5.3 Road 365 intersects with the National Recreation Trail. Follow the road around the bend to the right. Shortly, more views of the valley will begin to open up on the left. Stay on Road 365.

6.0 Pass through the saddle; continue climbing.

8.2 Road 365 crosses a creek.

9.3 Cross another creek.

11.5 There's a sign at the intersection of Roads 365 and 2137. Take a sharp left, through the gate, where the road deteriorates slightly; keep climbing.

12.8 At the nadir of a slight decline, Trail 605 intersects Road 2137; you'll return to this spot and descend the trail on your left if you're taking Deadman Gulch down Blue Mountain. Trail 605 is open to motorbikes and bicycles. It also runs uphill on a steep course to the Blue Mountain Lookout. Stay on Road 2137.

14.1 Take a sharp left, continuing uphill on the road leading to the lookout, only a couple hundred yards away.

14.4 Congratulations, you've made it! From the lookout, double back on the road.

14.7 As you descend, follow Road 2137 around a sharp right heading downhill; climb a short rise.

15.2 At the top of the rise, take a right onto Trail 605. Remember to look out for motorbikes. This is the beginning of a moderately technical, fairly steep descent. Obstacles include downed trees and loose rocks.

16.0 Continue on Trail 605, climbing briefly then descending, bearing left and keeping an eye out for drop-offs to the right for the next 0.25 mile.

16.5 Negotiate another short, steep climb. Obstacles over the next 2 miles of snaking singletrack include plenty of rubber water bars, roots, and loose rocks in the dirt.

18.4 The trail forks as Trail 607 splits off from Trail 605. Keep to the left on Trail 607, which rejoins Trail 605 after a little more than 0.1 mile.

18.7 Trail 607 intersects with Trail 605 again. Stay left, passing the motorcycle-difficulty rating sign posted at this fork. Return to Trail 605 for the next 0.2 mile.

18.9 Reach junction of Trails 605 and 602. Take a left onto Trail 602; continue descending.

19.5 Pass by the gate marked by the No Vehicles sign. This is private property, unfortunately, so stay out. Continue around to your left on Trail 602, taking the footbridge across Hayes Creek. Trail 602 intersects with Trail 603 just on the other side of the bridge.

19.7 Take a right onto Trail 603 and begin a short, fairly technical (Level 3) climb.

19.9 Near the top of this small hill, Trail 305 (pedestrians and horses only—no bikes) crosses Trail 603. Continue on Trail 603.

20.1 After a quick right turn on Trail 603, come to the junction with Trail 303. Take another right onto Trail 303 and begin descending through the woods over varied terrain.

20.3 Reach another junction with Trail 305. Stay on Trail 303 and continue descent, shortly emerging from the woods.

21.0 Although the terrain starts to smooth out, the trail network begins to get a little confusing here. Cutting across the hillside through parklike stands, Trail 303 comes upon a three-way fork. Do not take a left onto Trail 308! Continuing straight on Trail 307 or bearing right on Trail 304 will eventually return you to the horse-loading area and main trailhead. For simplicity and ease at this point, head right on Trail 304, which leads to an abandoned roadbed (if you need more singletrack, there's a nasty tire-width gully running parallel down the right side of this road).

21.5 Trails 310 and 309 join Trail 304 in succession. Continue descending on Trail 304. Be courteous to the other users you're likely to meet here!

22.2 Reach the fence that encloses the parking area. Welcome back!

Grizzly Creek Trail

Location: 30 miles east of Missoula and 12 miles up the Rock Creek drainage.

Distance: 6.1 miles to the top; 20.4 miles round-trip, including a jaunt to the spring.

Time: 45–90 minutes uphill; up to 2–3 hours round-trip.

Tread: Singletrack.

Aerobic level: Moderately strenuous.

Technical difficulty: Level 3-4 with some exposed and off-camber sections. The spring at the top is reached via a rutted Forest Service road with some minor ups and downs.

Highlights: Relative to many of the rides in the Missoula vicinity and Bitterroot Valley, the challenging Grizzly Creek Trail is a remote getaway where encounters with other trail users (outside hunting season) are extremely infrequent. The ride cuts up a wooded hillside away from the blue-ribbon trout stream Rock Creek, intersecting several times with Grizzly Creek. It eventually connects atop the Sapphire Mountain ridgeline with a network of Forest Service roads and trails in various states of maintenance, making this route a reasonable starting place for exploring a region rich in wildlife that also provides a change in scenery from many of the other rides discussed. A campsite at the start and area trails make this a worthwhile overnight if you have time. If you head south on the logging road at the ridge, a mountaintop spring a little more than another 4 miles away provides an additional turnaround point.

⊙•Grizzly Creek Trail

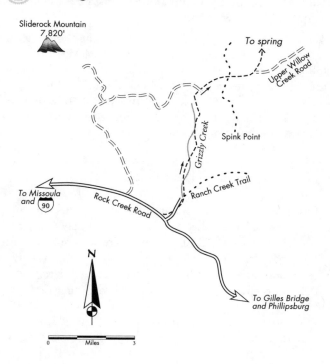

Sliderock Mountain
7,820'

To spring

Upper Willow
Creek Road

Spink Point

Grizzly Creek

Ranch Creek Trail

To Missoula
and 90

Rock Creek Road

To Gilles Bridge
and Phillipsburg

N

0   Miles   3

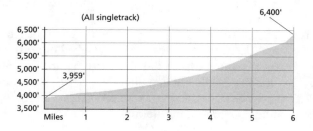

(All singletrack)

6,400'

3,959'

6,500'
6,000'
5,500'
5,000'
4,500'
4,000'
3,500'

Miles   1   2   3   4   5   6

Land status: Lolo National Forest.

Maps: USGS Grizzly Point, USGS Spink Point, and Lolo National Forest (west half).

Access: The trail starts 12 miles up the Rock Creek drainage, which is off I–90, 30 miles east of Missoula. Just follow the You'll Have A Ball signs to the Rock Creek Lodge, and continue south on Rock Creek Road until you see signs for Grizzly Creek and Ranch Creek Trails on your left. The parking area is just 0.25 mile or so off the main road, next to the Norton Campground.

The Ride

0.0 From the parking area follow the signs directing you to the trailheads for both the Grizzly Creek and Ranch Creek Trails. (Ranch Creek is strewn with boulders and next to impossible to ride from the bottom up, so it has not been included here.)

0.2 The singletrack broadens to reveal an overgrown jeep track.

0.5 Spot the sign for Grizzly Creek Trail 208 on your left; start into the woods on winding singletrack, paralleling Grizzly Creek. Shortly, up the hill to your left, you'll begin to see scree, which comes nearly to the trail's edge.

0.9 After a quick up and down, you ride across Grizzly Creek.

1.2 The hillside opens up to your right. Avoid the older trail on the right that has been blocked off; instead climb hard up the technical slope to your left. Keep climbing as the hill gets slightly easier to navigate.

1.6 Cross Grizzly Creek again. The next section is still a little technical, but the trail has been constructed relatively recently. Over the next 0.5 mile, you'll cross the creek twice more.

2.1 After crossing the creek a second time, keep climbing up and to your right until you find yourself dropping into a small gully. The trail is easy to see. Shortly you'll cross the creek again; bear right uphill to where the scree meets the trail.

2.4 Cross Grizzly Creek again and ride through the thick brush.

2.5 Reach a small clearing and a brief flat spot before continuing up the scree-covered trail.

2.6 The trail veers right into the trees, leaving behind the scree for a little while but forcing you to tackle some more thick brush. Soon the trail makes its way to the southern wall of the canyon.

2.9 A hard left carries you back toward the creek, and then the canyon begins to narrow. Trail conditions worsen; moss and thick brush may force you to walk awhile along Grizzly Creek.

3.2 Leaving the creek, find yourself on an exposed, technical section of trail as you return to the northern wall of the drainage.

3.5 Emerging from the trees at this point, the trail flattens out and narrows. Cutting across the grassy slope, the terrain is easier to manage but still slightly off-camber.

3.8 Take a sharp right, traversing the Grizzly Creek drainage to a west-facing slope. Get ready for a quick succession of switchbacks running and climbing perpendicular to the drainage over the next 0.25 mile.

4.2 Bear right as the trail straightens out and parallels the drainage then cuts back to the west-facing slope again.

4.8 Come to a fork in the trail. Take the left-hand path around the bend in the road, climbing until you enter the trees once again.

5.5 Bear left at this gully.

5.8 Take the first available right, following the meandering switchback as it keeps climbing up a slight grade through the trees. Soon you'll see the road and the ridgeline.

6.1 Top out at the road. An old metal GRIZZLY TRAIL sign nailed to the tree marks the path you've just been on. Enjoy the singing downhill, or continue south on the ridgeline to explore. There's a spring about 4 miles south of where you are now that's well worth the trip.

To the Spring

6.1 At the road take a right, heading southerly past the stock area.

7.0 Start a 0.5-mile climb.

8.2 Sign for the trail to Spink Point appears on your right; stay on the road.

8.4 Forest Service Road 8419 branches to your left; stay right. Road quality deteriorates.

10.2 A dirt road enters from the right; stay left. Keep an eye out for rocks and ruts, making the going a little rougher. The sign for the mountain spring is ahead, about 150 yards on the right. Follow the footpath to the spring. If conditions are wet, avoid riding your bike through the seasonal marsh. This is a great place to fill water bottles in the summer.

Lower Blue Mountain and Blue Mountain Motorized Loop

Location: Blue Mountain Recreation Area, 2 miles southwest of Missoula.

Distance: 8.3-mile loop.

Time: 45–90 minutes.

Tread: Singletrack, jeep trail, and short section on gravel road.

Aerobic level: Moderate–moderately strenuous.

Technical difficulty: Level 3–4.

Highlights: The system of trails at the Blue Mountain National Recreation Area is one of the first to dry out after the winter and provides a wide variety of options for beginners as well as expert mountain bikers. This section of trail is a Blue Mountain classic and provides an excellent introduction to what Blue Mountain has to offer at an intermediate level. Riding from downtown to Blue Mountain makes for an excellent workout, but the fast singletrack described herein can be tackled by those hoping to work on speed or skills or just looking for a quick blast between the end of the workday and dinner. Care should be taken, as some of the trails are shared with other users, including motorized ATVs and motorbikes, and other trails in this

•Lower Blue Mountain and Blue Mountain Motorized Loop

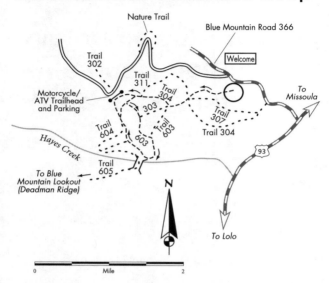

network are closed to bikes. Also keep an eye out during the shoulder seasons for deer, bear, and other wildlife.

Land status: Lolo National Forest.

Maps: USGS Southwest Missoula and USGS Blue Mountain. The Forest Service also has recreation area maps available at the trailhead.

Access: From Missoula travel 2 miles south of Reserve Street on Highway 93; turn right on Blue Mountain Road (County Road 30). Stay on Blue Mountain Road for 0.5 mile, where you'll find the horse-loading facilities and trailhead for the National Recreational Trail (bikes are prohibited). Continue about another 0.25 mile on Blue Mountain Road, bearing left at Road 365, which leads to the main entrance and a small parking area. I describe the ride starting here.

The Ride

0.0 Directly across from the Blue Mountain WELCOME sign, just beyond the cattle guard, a gate blocks cars from entering an old jeep trail. A sign designates this as Trail 308; start riding here.

0.2 Stay on the old wagon road as it winds around to the right and the slope gets steeper, and then around to the left.

0.5 Trail 308 intersects with the doubletrack that is the National Recreation Trail 301. Take a right, staying on 308, which flattens out shortly.

1.0 Trail 308 comes to a junction with Trail 309; the signs are confusing here. Continue on Trail 308, going straight uphill and not changing direction at any of the alternative trails cutting across the hillside.

1.5 Conditions deteriorate as you continue uphill, veering left past a rocky outcropping.

1.6 Trail 308 intersects with Trails 304 and 307. Take a right onto Trail 304, the wide gravel road.

1.7 A sketchy singletrack enters from the left; stay right on Trail 304.

1.8 At a signed intersection, Trail 303 splits off to the left from Trail 304. Continue straight on Trail 304; also bypass the intersection with Trail 305. (This, too, is signed—note that Trail 305 is closed to cyclists.)

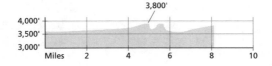

2.2 Come to the signed intersection of Trails 304 and 311, which enters from below. Trail 311 is also closed to bikes; continue straight on Trail 304.

2.5 There should be a gate directly in front of you. Pass this on the right, which should deposit you on Road 365. Although Trail 302 directly across the road from you looks inviting, it, too, is closed to bikes. Instead take a left at the elbow in the road, and enter the motorcycle/ATV parking area and trailhead.

2.7 Ride through the parking lot and onto the trail, bearing left as you go around the fence and hit the singletrack. Keep your eyes peeled for Trail 311 entering from the left (the short section of Trail 311 just below where you are now to its junction with Trail 304 is open to bikes). Take a right at this intersection, picking up Trail 603.

3.2 Trail 303 (open to bikes) joins 603 from the left. Continue straight on Trail 603, and get ready to begin your decent. In another 0.1 mile, Trail 305 (closed to bikes) also enters from the left. Stick to Trail 603, which drops quickly for the next 0.5 mile to Hayes Creek and a junction with Trails 602 and 604.

4.6 Take your first right—this should be signed as Trail 602 (closed to motor vehicles)—and begin a steep, snaking, and mildly technical climb back to the motorcycle/ATV trailhead. Do not cross the creek here, although Trail 602 on the other side connects to Deadman Gulch (see Ride 15).

4.9 Be careful at this intersection between Trails 602 and 604 as you reach the top of the hill because motorized travel is allowed on Trail 604. Continue back to the motorcycle/ATV trailhead.

5.0 Follow the fenceline at the parking lot around to your right. Back through the trees you can take in a nice view of the Bitterroots. Follow Trail 603 to its intersection with Trail 303 and veer to the left on Trail 303. The upcoming short descent is full of minor technical challenges.

5.3 Go right on the singletrack to the signed junction of Trails 303 and 311. Take a right on Trail 311.

5.6 Take another right at the signed junction of Trails 311 and 304. Go right on Trail 304 and continue descent for another mile.

6.6 Go right on Trail 304 as it intersects with Trails 307 (no bikes) and 308.

7.0 Take a left on Trail 304 where Trail 309 (no bikes) enters from the right. Descend on the road or the rutted singletrack just to the right of the road to the horse-loading area and main trailhead.

7.5 For the simplest way to return to the main entrance for Blue Mountain from the main trailhead for the National Recreation Trail and horse-loading area, take a left on the gravel-surfaced Blue Mountain Road, heading west. (For an off-road return to the main entrance, see alternative that follows.)

8.3 Go left at the intersection, leaving Blue Mountain Road and arriving on Road 365. Ride over the cattle guard, pass the WELCOME sign, and return to your vehicle.

Alternative Return

7.5 Take a left before the horse-loading area onto singletrack Trail 309, climbing a slight rise.

7.8 Go left as Trail 309 turns to doubletrack, and continue on Trail 309 to its intersection with Trail 307 (signed NO BIKES), entering from the right. Bear left again at the upcoming fork.

8.0 Bear right on Trail 309.

8.2 Trail 309 intersects with Trail 308. Take right onto Trail 308 and begin winding descent on old jeep road. Stay on Trail 308 at its intersection with Trail 301, the National Recreation Trail (no bikes), and follow the road back down the way you came.

8.6 Reach gate and main entrance to Blue Mountain National Recreation Area. A left on Road 365 returns to parking area.

Blackfoot River Railroad Grade

Location: Along the Blackfoot River, 20 miles north of Missoula.

Distance: 8.7 miles round-trip.

Time: 45–90 minutes.

Tread: Mostly doubletrack and jeep roads on the way out, with improved road on the return.

Aerobic level: Easy.

Technical difficulty: Level 1–2 with a couple of more challenging spots.

•Blackfoot River Railroad Grade

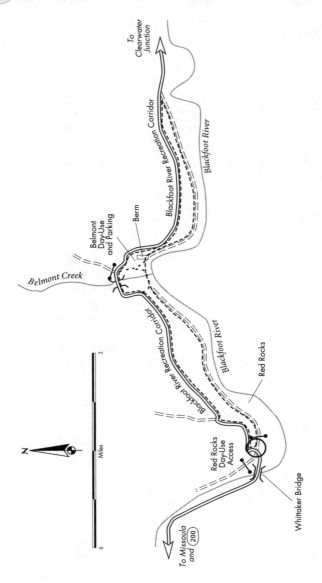

Highlights: The Blackfoot River Recreation Corridor is primarily used by boaters and anglers. This ride offers plenty of the same scenic pleasures as you follow an old railroad bed upriver, tracing the route of not just steam engines but also the region's Native American tribes. Famous Missoula author Norman Maclean wrote of this section of river in his classic, *A River Runs Through It*. It's a relatively easy route, appropriate to beginners, with swimming and plenty of river access along the way that experienced riders looking for exercise can combine with the more challenging out-and-back route described in Ride 19. On the return for this ride, beware of traffic, especially logging trucks. During summer the road gets lots of weekend motorized use and tends to be prohibitively dusty.

Land status: Bureau of Land Management.

Maps: USGS Potomac.

Access: Head north from Missoula on Highway 200 for 12 miles, taking a right at the sign for the Blackfoot River Recreation Corridor and continuing along the river-access road for a few miles until you reach Whittacker Bridge. The road is rough, but clearance should not be a problem for most vehicles. Park on the far side of the bridge, either under the trees on the far bank of the river or at the parking area just before the bend after you cross the river. Be mindful of the gates and the NO PARKING signs next to the bridge. You could be ticketed otherwise. There's also parking just around the bend after the bridge at the Red Rocks day-use area.

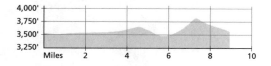

The Ride

0.0 Leaving the parking area, take a left on the road, heading toward Whittacker Bridge, and a second quick left at the gate across the railroad grade, which bears a NO PARKING sign. Hop the fence.

0.1 Set off down the railroad grade, a flat pebbled track with plenty of loose rocks. On your right, a footpath to the popular Red Rocks swimming area should be visible through the trees.

0.5 The woods open up to provide a view of the Blackfoot River and the Red Rocks beach.

1.0 Pass a pile of rocks on your left; the river should still be visible on your right. Keep going straight for the next mile, leaving the woods behind and enjoying the plateau above the river.

2.1 A couple of healthy dirt berms mark the approach to Belmont Creek; you will have to dismount to cross. A narrow path heads down into the gully, or you can hike about 40 yards up the hill to your left and hop on the road for about 0.25 mile. At the height of spring runoff, don't even bother with the angler's footpath. As you come around the oxbow on the road, continue straight ahead to the well-marked Belmont Creek day-use area. The trail branches to the left about 200 yards below the parking area, just above the river. Watch for traffic if you're using the road.

2.2 Remount bike. A berm forces the singletrack to the right. Be careful around this drop-off!

2.4 The path cuts across the grade prior to a second berm. Continue up and over this pile of dirt. On the other side it's a rider's choice between the railroad bed or the nearby angler's path down the slope to the riverbank on your right. Up to your left see the recreation road; continue straight ahead.

2.8 There's a fenced-off field to your left. Continue paralleling the river along this bench.

3.4 The road connecting the railroad grade to the Blackfoot Recreation Road enters the bench; its edge is marked by small piles of stone.

3.7 The railroad grade merges with the road at the end of the fence, where there's a DAY-USE ONLY sign. Take a left here onto the road to return to Whittaker Bridge via the Blackfoot Recreation Road. Or double back on the railroad grade the way you came.

3.8 Road conditions improve as the ride ascends 1 mile along the recreation road—keep a look out for traffic in both directions!

4.8 Begin descent to the oxbow over Belmont Creek.

5.2 Take a right turn, following the sign with an arrow for Johnsrud Campground. To your left is the Belmont Creek day-use area and the path that leads to the river. Stay on the recreation road and begin climbing.

5.7 There's a gated road off to your right. Bear left, descending once again.

5.9 The oxbow reaches the bridge over Belmont Creek; you'll pass a pair of roads your right heading up the mountain—the first has no gate; the second is gated. Continue on the Blackfoot Recreation Road for a little over another 0.5 mile until you reach the Belmont Creek overlook.

6.6 At the Belmont Creek overlook, continue on the recreation road—although, the intrepid may want to descend to the Blackfoot River and return to Whittaker Bridge along the railroad grade. Staying on the road carries you off and away from the river.

7.7 Continue climbing for another 0.25 mile, staying on the recreation road and passing another pair of logging roads to your right. The Blackfoot is visible below to your left through much of this section.

7.9 After passing the second logging road on your right, begin the final descent to the parking areas and Whittaker Bridge.

8.4 The parking area for Red Rocks day-use area is on your left.

8.7 Bear left around the bend and see the parking area.

Blackfoot Recreation Corridor Overlook

Location: Along the Blackfoot River, 20 miles north of Missoula.

Distance: 4.8 miles one-way.

Time: 30–60 minutes to the top.

Tread: Out-of-use logging roads and some doubletrack.

Aerobic level: Moderate–moderately difficult.

Technical difficulty: Level 2–3.

Highlights: The Blackfoot River Recreation Corridor is primarily used by boaters and anglers, but this ride offers plenty of the same scenic pleasures that draw these recreationists.

Blackfoot Recreation Corridor Overlook

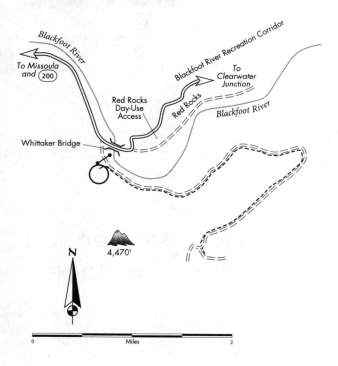

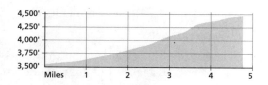

In contrast with the railroad grade across the river (see Ride 18), this route departs the river bottom quickly and provides a chance to do some serious climbing. It's an out-and-back ride that will carry you high above the valley floor before the road eventually becomes so overgrown that continuing will be an option only for the most dedicated explorers. Honestly, the overlook is not the most scenic in the region, but that keeps the area from being too exploited. Special care should be taken during hunting season; few people venture up this way, so game is abundant, including a variety of birds, deer, elk, and the occasional bear or coyote. If you want to combine this with Ride 18, I recommend tackling this ride first.

Land status: Bureau of Land Management, State of Montana, and Plum Creek Timber Company.

Maps: USGS Potomac.

Access: Head north from Missoula on Highway 200 for 12 miles, taking a right at the sign for the Blackfoot River Recreation Corridor and continuing along the river-access road for a few miles until you reach Whittacker Bridge. The road is rough, but clearance should not be a problem for most vehicles. Park on the far side of the bridge, either under the trees on the far bank of the river or at the parking area just before the bend after you cross the river. Be mindful of the gates and the NO PARKING signs next to the bridge. You could be ticketed otherwise.

The Ride

0.0 On the southeast side of the river, just above Whittaker Bridge, head north from the gate with the NO PARKING sign, leaving behind the Blackfoot Recreation Road and paralleling the river from afar on its eastside.

0.1 Pass a rock outcropping on your right and begin gradual ascent. The road here is still in fairly good condition.

0.4 Descend briefly.

0.6 This section of road is rocky and rutted, but it shortly emerges as a smooth path cutting through a pine forest struggling to regenerate itself.

1.0 Up to your left across the Blackfoot, the recreation road is visible cutting across the hillside.

1.4 Begin climbing for a little more than 0.5 mile.

2.0 The road descends into a valley that still shows signs of logging.

2.4 The road turns into doubletrack as it starts climbing once again.

2.8 Views of the Blackfoot River lie below to the left; the whole valley opens up directly in front of you for picturesque views. Stay on the road, riding over rolling hills for the next mile.

3.8 Make a sharp right. Bypass various hollows as you climb up doubletrack overgrown with grass. As you head uphill, great views of the Blackfoot River Valley emerge to the south.

4.8 Reach a good turnaround point as a left turn deposits you on a promontory with more views across the valley to the north and south. The trail forks here as well. The trail on your left is overgrown with brush but rises and falls, eventually returning to the Blackfoot drainage. Take a right and you can keep climbing to the eastern ridgeline. Heading back the way you came is the easiest option. (If you haven't had enough, see Ride 18, or consider riding along the Blackfoot River Recreation Corridor for a while.)

Sheep Mountain

Location: Northeast of Missoula, connecting Mount Jumbo and Rattlesnake National Recreation Area.

Distance: 26.8-mile loop.

Time: 5–8 hours.

Tread: Singletrack, doubletrack, and jeep and gravel roads.

Aerobic level: Very strenuous.

Technical difficulty: 3–4 plus.

Highlights: This is the definitive Missoula ride, traveling the ridgelines high above two valleys to the highest peaks in the Rattlesnake National Recreation Area and then dropping down through mixed terrain of conifer forests and beargrass to the main stem of the Rattlesnake Trail System just north of Franklin Bridge. Because of the remote country the path traverses, the length of the trail, and the overall difficulty of this ride, only the strongest riders will want to tackle the course I describe here in one day. A logging road through Plum Creek Timber Company land on the Highway 200 corridor at Gold Creek provides additional access—check with any of the local bike shops or riding organizations for details—but for those looking to bag a peak from the valley floor, there is no better way to go than the way I've laid things out here. Along the way, keep your eyes open for mountain lions, black and possibly grizzly bears, elk, deer, and more.

•Sheep Mountain

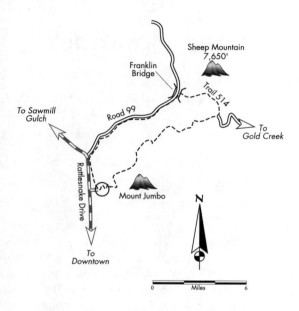

Sheep Mountain
7,650'

Franklin
Bridge

Trail 514

To Sawmill
Gulch

Road 99

To
Gold Creek

Rattlesnake Drive

Mount Jumbo

N

To
Downtown

0   Miles   6

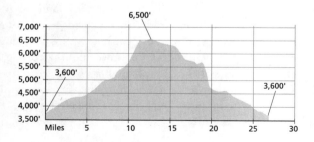

Land status: Lolo National Forest, Rattlesnake National Recreation Area, Plum Creek Timber Company land, City of Missoula, and Missoula County.

Maps: USGS Northeast Missoula, USGS Blue Point, and Lolo National Forest.

Access: To get to the Mount Jumbo entrance by car or bike, take Rattlesnake Drive north of I–90 for about a mile and take a right on Lincoln Hills Drive. Follow this road as it winds to the hilltop, where you'll see the access for the city's open space lands at the top of Mount Jumbo. I recommend leaving a car at the Rattlesnake National Recreation Area main trailhead or arranging a shuttle from there, as you will not want to climb this hill after conquering Sheep Mountain. While I have described this ride as a point-to-point incomplete loop, you can descend the mountain the way you came. There is some parking at the Mount Jumbo access.

The Ride

0.0 Accessing the ride from the top of Lincoln Hills Drive, ride due north from the Mount Jumbo access gate, which has an area map and signs, on rutted doubletrack.

0.1 Bear right at the fork, heading east by northeast and climbing to the saddle of Mount Jumbo on this doubletrack for the next mile.

1.1 Take another right at the fork just beyond the saddle, heading toward the Clark Fork River Valley (a left will carry you up a trying ascent to the top of Woods Gulch).

1.3 Descend to gate, entering from Marshall Grade (see Rides 1 and 7); take the stairs on the right of this access point. Start riding on gravel logging road.

1.4 Bear left at fork, ascending on well-maintained dirt road above the valley. Stay on this road for the next 0.9 mile.

2.3 Pass through the remnants of a wooden gate. Keep climbing for nearly 2 more miles.

3.7 Views of Marshall Mountain Ski Area lie below to your right.

3.9 Bear left as road bends left; climb.

4.2 Stay on road. Note singletrack on your left; this trail leads back to access for Woods Gulch and the saddle of Mount Jumbo.

4.6 Stick to the high trail on the right and keep climbing.

5.0 The grade flattens out briefly, then ascent continues.

5.2 Follow road around sharp right.

6.1 As you pass through this drainage and over a small gully, stay on the road. Views of the Missoula Valley can be seen behind on your right side.

6.3 Stay right and keep climbing as the road splits, with one track heading sharply to the left.

6.7 Take the singletrack section directly ahead through the woods. The road will eventually lead to Woods Gulch, but this route is a shortcut to Sheep Mountain.

6.8 Bear left at the intersection. The trail begins to get more technical, charging over rocks, roots, and the occasional water bar.

7.4 Descend the singletrack to your left (the path straight in front here is next to impossible to bike).

8.1 Bear right around the elbow in the path. Views of Missoula and the Bitterroot Mountains are visible due south. The trail gets much more technical over the next 0.75 mile.

8.8 Emerge from tree line.

9.1 Cross upper saddle for next 0.5 mile.

9.7 Descend on trail to your left. See Blue Point in that direction as you reach an intersection with the roads from Marshall Mountain. Look out for dead-fall and other obstacles! This is rough going.

10.0 Negotiate a tough, rocky, technical climb.

10.2 The trail turns to rolling singletrack for nearly a mile.

11.1 Resume climbing on gradual but technical ridgeline trail.

12.4 Go straight past the washed-out singletrack descent, following the East Fork of Rattlesnake Creek. Continue climbing; the first summit is ahead of you.

12.8 Reach the primary summit overlooking Wicherd Ridge, a popular backcountry ski destination, and follow the trail around the face of the point, taking the first trail on your right. The coming terrain drops along a technical section that is very rocky and exposed!

13.2 Resume climbing the singletrack to the Sheep Mountain summit.

13.3 As you reach the trail's highest point, you can leave your bike on the trail and head for the old lookout on the peak for a breather.

13.5 Head on Trail 513 for the north face of Sheep Mountain and begin descending along the rocky switch-backs for the next mile.

14.4 Reach the tree line and continue descending. The trail gets less technical as you enter the woods.

15.8 Go straight, passing a drop-off trail along the East Fork of Rattlesnake Creek to your left. The trail ceases losing altitude, flattening out momentarily then climbing briefly through the trees.

16.0 Reach intersection of Trail 513 and a doubletrack spur from Gold Creek Road.

16.2 Bear right, traversing the hillside on the doubletrack.

16.6 Go left onto singletrack and continue descent.

16.8 Take steep, left-handed drop—be careful of obstacles!

17.1 Bear right at on East Fork Rattlesnake Trail 514, which reaches another junction with Trail 513.

17.3 Crisscross the creek four times over the next 0.25 mile. Steep drops and mud under wet conditions add to the challenge of this section. The trail narrows as it descends.

18.0 Cross the creek; climb over technical section of roots and rocks, entering a stand of burned wood and plenty of beargrass and other brushy vegetation, which goes on for about 0.25 mile.

18.3 The trail intersects Mineral Creek Trail 511. Continue straight and drop into the next drainage.

18.7 Dropping, cross creek bed and continue descent for about a mile. The terrain here is intermediate with some deadfall, rocks, and exposed roots.

19.4 As you return to the main Rattlesnake Trail, you'll parallel a creek on your left for about 0.5 mile.

19.9 Reach the Rattlesnake Main Trail (Road 99; see Ride 5), just above Franklin Bridge; take a left and continue descending along this rocky road.

20.2 Bear right, crossing the cement Franklin Bridge over Rattlesnake Creek, then bear left.

22.0 Following the rocky and undulating road, reach Beeskove Creek, a tributary of Rattlesnake Creek.

25.0 There's a Forest Service outhouse on your left as you enter the 3-mile zone (no camping between here and the trailhead).

25.8 Continue straight past the singletrack spur on your right. A small wooden sign indicates that this is the Wallman Trail and Spring Gulch Trail (see Ride 6) heading northwest from here.

26.0 Stay on the main road, passing singletrack and an outhouse on your left.

26.2 Emerge from the woods; stay on Road 99, avoiding singletrack on your right then left.

26.5 As the valley opens up, you'll see the pack bridge on your left (no bikes) and intersections with various trails on your right. Continue descending the main trail, which flattens out as you come to the bottom of the Rattlesnake National Recreation Area.

26.6 Continue straight on the Rattlesnake Main Trail to the parking lot, passing brush on your left, paralleling the creek, and a rock wall on your right.

26.8 Reach the Rattlesnake Main trailhead and parking lot.

Appendix A

Other Missoula Area Rides

I have not mapped these rides outright for this volume, but they are popular routes that can be combined with those in this book or done on their own. I'm indebted to Missoula's bike shops, the Forest Service and Bureau of Land Management, Adventure Cycling, and Low Impact Bicyclists of Missoula for helping round up these recommendations. Since I have not personally ridden most of these tracks, I have left them intentionally vague. I recommend getting a more complete description from one of the above sources before heading out.

Marshall Canyon Road

This climb can be approached from a variety of points and provides access to Mount Jumbo and Woods Gulch from the east. It can be combined with any of the rides that involve climbing Mount Jumbo from downtown, including Ride 20 up Sheep Mountain, offering a strenuous but intermediate-level grade up gravel logging roads. To get to the base of the road, drive or bike to East Missoula and follow Old Highway 10 approximately 1 mile north to signs for the Marshall Mountain Ski Area. Take a left, heading northwest up Marshall Canyon Road a little more than a mile and turn onto the gated logging road Number 2122. At the top you can choose between riding across to the saddle of Mount Jumbo, hooking up with Woods Gulch, or continuing to climb along logging roads until you connect with the Sheep Mountain Trail. Bottom to top and back again should take one to two hours. Maps include USGS Northeast Missoula, USGS Blue Point, and Lolo National Forest.

Kreis Pond Trails

The Ninemile Ranger District, about 25 miles west of Missoula (halfway to the small town of Alberton out I–90), offers nearly 35 miles of trails around Kreis Pond. The rides this way tend to be easy to intermediate and are generally way less crowded than those close into town. Some routes are open to motorized traffic, so beware of cars. As always, respect private property. The easiest mountain bike trail is the 2.3-mile so-called Yellow Trail, which circles the pond. More serious riders will want to attempt the 14.6-mile Red Trail, which follows Ninemile and Butler Creeks and offers more narrow, technical trails. The pond has a population of trout and largemouth bass, and there are eight picnic sites there as well. To get to Kreis Pond, take exit 82 off I–90 and take Remount Road north past the ranger station, where you can find trail maps (maps are always available at Forest Service headquarters in Missoula). From the ranger station, take Road 456 until it intersects with Road 2176, which takes you to Kreis Pond.

Cyr Flat Figure "8"

Start at Big Pine Campground, which contains the biggest ponderosa pine in Montana, and enjoy a moderate 19-mile loop on primitive roads west of Missoula. Nice views of the Alberton Gorge, a scenic section of the Clark Fork River, can be had during the first part of this ride; elevation gains are only about 300 feet. Allow at least two hours to complete the entire ride, which is described in detail in Adventure Cycling's guide to mountain biking missoula. To get there, travel 38 miles west of Missoula on I–90 and take exit 66, crossing over the interstate and following BIG PINE CAMPGROUND signs.

Garnet Mountain Trails

In addition to the loops described in this guide (see Ride 8), the Garnet Range Bureau of Land Management office has mapped dozens of miles of improved mountaintop roads that are available for exploration. This is remote country, generally not traveled much, so while the rides are not extremely difficult, make sure you have proper tools and supplies. Many of the routes follow high ridges, meaning weather can change fast, but the rewards include remarkable mountain views and plenty of wildlife. Those looking for more challenging ups and downs will want to tackle either Cave Gulch Road or Bear Gulch, which both provide access to the Garnet Ghost Town parking area from I–90 (take either the Bearmouth or Drummond exit), but watch for vehicles on these steep roads. The Garnet Range Road can also be reached from Highway 200, about 30 miles east of Missoula. The Bureau of Land Management offers maps showing various routes at the Garnet Ghost Town Visitor Center.

The Willow Creek Loop

Instead of riding the short Grizzly Creek Trail (see Ride 16) out Rock Creek way east of Missoula, try the Willow Creek Loop, which starts and finishes at Norton Campground and covers 60+ miles. Most riders will want to stretch this trip overnight (trust me, I did it in one day and barely survived). During the height of summer, you'll only want to try it during the week; on weekends, the dust raised by anglers on Rock Creek Road is inescapable. The folks at Adventure Cycling recommend tackling this by starting south along Rock Creek from Norton Campground, which carries you toward Phillipsburg until you reach Gilles Bridge. Then take a left onto Willow Creek Road, eventually climbing past Spink Point and Sliderock Mountain before descending Brewster Creek. Although it's not too technical, due to its distance this ride is not for the meek. Be sure to bring plenty of water, food, and supplies.

Appendix B

Information Sources

Public Lands Agencies

Forest Service Region 1 Headquarters
200 East Broadway
P.O. Box 7669
Missoula, MT 59807
(406) 329–3511

Lolo National Forest Office
Fort Missoula, Building 24
Missoula, MT 59804
(406) 329–3750

Bitterroot National Forest Office
1801 North First Street
Hamilton, MT 59840
(406) 363–7161

Missoula Ranger District
Fort Missoula, Building 24-A
Missoula, MT 59804
(406) 329–3750

Ninemile Ranger District
20325 Remount Road
Huson, MT 59846
(406) 626–5201

Darby Ranger Station
712 North Main Street
Darby, MT 59829
(406) 821–3913

Bureau of Land Management, Missoula Office
3255 Fort Missoula Road
Missoula, MT 59801
(406) 329–3914

Montana Fish, Wildlife & Parks Department
3201 Spurgin Road
Missoula, MT 59801
(406) 542–5500

Missoula Parks and Recreation Department
100 Hickory Street
Missoula, MT 59801
(406) 721–7275

Local Conservation Advocates

Five Valleys Land Trust
211 North Higgins Avenue, Suite 4A
Missoula, MT 59802
(406) 549–0755

Save Open Space
1916 Brooks Street, PMB 352
Missoula, MT 59801
(406) 549–6083

Cycling Groups

Low Impact Mountain Bicyclists (LIMB)
P.O. Box 2896
Missoula, MT 59806
limb@limb.org (no phone)

Adventure Cycling Association
150 East Pine Street
P.O. Box 8308
Missoula, MT 59807
(406) 721–1776

International Mountain Biking Association (IMBA)
1121 Broadway, Suite 203
P.O. Box 7578
Boulder, CO 80306
(303) 545–9011
Toll-free (888) 442–4622

Bike Shops

Bicycle Hanger
1801 Brooks Street
Missoula, MT 59801
(406) 728–9537

Big Sky Cyclery
1110 South Avenue West
Missoula, MT 59801
(406) 543–3331

Bike Doctor
420 Higgins Avenue
Missoula, MT 59802
(406) 721–5357

Bitterroot Bicycle Works
176 South Second Street
Hamilton, MT 59840
(406) 363–0665

Missoula Bicycle Works
113 Main Street
Missoula, MT 59802
(406) 721–6525

Open Road Bicycles
517 South Orange Street
Missoula, MT 59801
(406) 549–2453